Her Ebony Glory

A Tribute to My Sisters Of Color

By
Juli Jasinski

Foreword by Bishop Sarah Jackson
Apostolic Life Center Church
Marvell, Arkansas

All scripture quotations are from the King James Bible unless otherwise stated

God's beautiful ladies for the cover of this book:
Lena Barry (mom) and Alexis Barry (daughter) of POK, Katy Texas. Photograph taken by Sara Hodge, Owner of
Simple Extravagence Photography 1 (832) 451-2129
Check her out on FACEBOOK

Cover design by Laura Merchant, PPH

Printed in the United States of America

ISBN 0-9650467-5-3

For more information on Juli Jasinski's other materials or to schedule a speaking engagement contact or visit her website:

www.Julisbooks.com

Juli Jasinski
31 No. Pepperell Road
Hollis, NH 03049
(603) 557-2071
Pwrxtrem2aol.com

Table of Contents

Other works by Juli Jasinski

My Hair My Glory

Daring Dos

Mi Pelo, Mi Gloria

My Hair My Glory—DVD
MHMG Seminar Workbook

Christian Soldiers Workshop
Soul Winner's Boot Camp Training
TEACHER ADDITION
STUDENTS WORKBOOK
POWERPOINT SLIDES (DVD)

Acknowledgements

* *Thank you Jesus for helping me share the love you have for your women of color.*

* *Thank you to my hubby, Stan Jasinski, you're so wonderful and Andrew, you are my joy.*

* *Thank you to all the ladies who kept me going on this project. Without your help I'd never got it done. Sarah Jackson, Brenda Chase, Betty Crawford*

* *Evangelist Carlton Clark, thanks for the insights*

* *Thank you to Leslie Owen who checked over this work.*

* *Thank you to Sara Hodge with Simple Extravagence Photography and letting God use your talent.*

* *Thank you to God's beautiful ladies for the cover of this book: Lena Barry (mom) and Alexis Barry (daughter) of POK Katy Texas.*

Pastor Sarah Jackson

Foreword

The age-old problem for the women of color has been *"What can I do with my hair?"* Whether it is natural, hot pressed or chemically treated to become straight, it has been, and for the most part still is, a struggle. Many women of color have resorted to bobbed hair from one-half inch to one inch in length to avoid the hassles of trying to keep a hairstyle. However, we who have biblical knowledge know that women should not cut their hair.

For years, because of the difference in the texture of the hair of the "average" African-American woman, it has been difficult for her to stay within the trends of what is called a "GOOD Hairdo." Most of the advertisements have been geared to the Caucasian women. Seemingly, all of the tips for having healthy hair did not meet the need of the woman of color. Therefore, when she tried the advertised products, it did not work because the texture of her hair needed more than what was offered. This has been a source of frustration for many African-American women.

For this cause, I am thankful for this book, ***Her Ebony Glory*** by Sister Juli Jasinski. She has done extensive research to show the historical Diaspora and how it relates to the struggles of the African-American woman's dilemma concerning her hair. In this book, she gives many tips for maintaining the health and growth of the "tightly curled" hair type which is typical for the African-American woman. After all, her hair is her glory, too. Not only has she given history and tips, but she has also given an exhaustive list of authors and resources concerning this subject.

Sister Jasinski and I have been friends for many years, and I know her to be diligent in what she does. As in her first book, ***My Hair, My Glory,*** she has been as diligent in researching and writing this book ***Her Ebony Glory*** for women of color. This truly is a tribute to sisters of color.

As an Apostolic African-American, female preacher for over twenty years, it is a pleasure and an honor to know Sister Juli Jasinski and to write the foreword for her new book.

Reverend Sarah Jackson
Founder and Pastor
Apostolic Life Center Church and
Christian Academy, Marvell, Arkansas

Preface

This book has been long in the making, by that I mean, I've put off writing it long enough. And even though I've seemingly put it off, it's not been for reasons that I didn't want to deal with the issue. It was because other pressing things got in the way. And now as Evangelist Shirley Ceasear would sing, *"It's your turn now... to be blessed."* And truly I hope that this book will bless you, my dear sisters of color.

My idea for this book, *Her Ebony Glory* was borne out of a burden for Apostolic African-American (AAA) sisters. As I stood and watched how my first book ***"My Hair, My Glory-Is There Really Any Significance,"*** sold at conferences and seminars, I noticed how you did not pick up the book. Perhaps you would glance down at it but never pick it up. I was perplexed. You'd look at the front cover then pass it by. I began to wonder why. What was the reason for you to disregard my book? After all, you had glory on your head! Then one day it dawned on me; my first book did not meet your needs as a godly woman of color.

Year after year, the whole scene played over and over in my mind as to why the Apostolic African-American sister would not pick up and read my book. And this bothered me. Then it hit me like a ton of bricks. I began to inquire with some of my black sister friends.

Later, I did some investigative footwork on my own. It wasn't long until I discovered some very interesting and pertinent facts about you, your history and culture. The things I learned were very fascinating.

Her Ebony Glory

I always believed that God made black ladies (AAA) beautiful. Your skin is so smooth and your hair so soft. In no time at all, I was made to understand that what we are dealing with is an ultra sensitive issue here. And very abruptly I found out that long hair is offensive to you. The average person doesn't realize this. Hair is the very touchstone of your heart, the very essence of your being.

Many times when I was knee deep in my research, a flood of tears ran down my face stopping me from my studying. God had revealed to me that hair to you was more than just *hair*; it was your *everything*. Is it not true? Your culture, your identity, and your self-image are all wrapped up in your hair.

But then I thought to myself, that's not all that different for any other woman on this planet. Then like a scroll the drama unfolded before my eyes. You've not only been fighting this hair dilemma for years but throughout generations.

The weight of the burden to write this book was heavy upon my heart. I just spent eight thousand dollars and two years researching "hair" in general. But your need was greater than what my first two books covered.

Finally, I reached the top of convincing facts, 633 articles to be exact and numerous books (at least 50). I even decided to make a personal visit to the beautiful Howard University in Washington, DC, (college for African-Americans) to further my studies on this issue.

After this entire endeavor, uncovering gobs of information, unlocking the mystery of hair and the black woman, I thought it was time to write out what I found. I believe it is God's timing for this attempt to help us all understand the dynamics of the African-American woman's hair as it relates to

us, Jesus Name Oneness Apostolics, holders of truth. It's your time to find out what the truth is about your ebony glory. And it's pretty awesome!

I wanted to have some close counsel so I asked a few sanctified black sisters who are dear friends, women pastors, singers, and pastor's wives what is the deal about hair. Some AAA brothers had some say too, they said that they were at a lost about talking of hair to their ladies. AAA women helped me sympathize with what you've gone through with your hair, and yes, are still going through now today. I've learned that your hair has special needs and requirements.

We will explain the whole anatomy of your hair in this book. But first, we will discuss your ebony glory through historical accounts (dispelling racial lies) then offer some suggestions to you, the reader, so that you may rediscover God's intended-will for your life as you let your glory shine.

This book offers some hope and some solid answers. Finally, because the research was so exhaustive, (I was the one exhausted), I will be referring to some excellent books on hair [care] for black women.

My sole desire is to minister to you through this book. It is my prayer that God touches you with a refreshed feeling and a deep inner healing. If you should come away with anything that is a blessing let God get all the glory.

It would be a joy to know that you found your hair is truly God's glory upon you and it's your authoritative power to do combat with the wicked one. So let it shine!

It would be a joy to know that you found your hair is truly God's glory upon you and it's your authoritative power to do combat with the wicked one. ***So let it shine!***

That's a secret the devil was hoping you'd never find out…but it's too late. God has let the truth be known. Now go, take back what the devil has stole. He can't keep your glory from shining.

This book is my tribute to you…as the song says; "Red and yellow, black and white, they are precious in His sight…" Precious you are, to Him and the body of Christ. May God richly bless you as you read this book.

Respectfully yours,

Juli Jasinski

Introduction

When I saw our black sisters walk by the book table at conferences where **"My Hair, My Glory"** book lay, I wondered what turned them away. What could they be thinking? There must be a reason why they would not lean over to pick up a copy?

Before all this, some of my friends of color told me that for the common African-American lady, her hair doesn't grow but about a few inches or so per year. I thought, "really, that's strange, then why doesn't it grow?" All these questions came to my mind. How come some sister's hair won't grow out? And why would God Almighty, Creator of the heavens and earth have the Apostle Paul write an edict in the Bible that one third of the women wouldn't be capable to apply in their lives?

The Scripture says in First Corinthians 11:15 ***"But if a woman have long hair, it is a glory to her: for her hair is given her for a covering."*** Sweet Jesus, how can women who are of an African decent have this long hair if theirs doesn't grow? More questions began to burn in my mind. We've got a problem. I couldn't shake the thoughts. God was about to show me what was going on and give an answer to this problem. (Praise God!)

I know I heard brothers preach that the definition of "long hair" doesn't necessarily mean the length of your hair it just means, "uninterrupted." And through much research on my part, I can confirm that claim. Indeed it does mean that. So it is understood that "uninterrupted" means a woman should not <u>interrupt the growth of her hair</u>. A good example of this is when a man visits the barber; he interrupts the growth of his hair by getting his hair cut. We'll discuss the details later. If you can't wait, see my other book, *Daring Dos*, *page 8* for a detailed definition of long.

Well ok, that is fine and dandy, but for somebody just to have a knowledge of a Biblical definition of the word "long" doesn't solve the dilemma that our black sisters wrestle with daily. I must be honest I was a little confused myself. I had to get on my face before God and cry out for some real answers. There must be some kind of logical explanation.

One day I got to praying on my knees and crying out to Jesus. Please understand I wasn't trying to be disrespectful to Jesus in how I worded my questions. I just had a desperate plead. (I heard one time that a starving man has no manners). So here is what I said to the Lord, *"How can a God who is so great and awesome, command us women of God to have uncut, glorious hair and keep it long when my sisters of color can not even grow an inch of hair on their head per year? How can this be fair, God? Why can't they measure up to the Scripture? How can you do this to them?"*

I kept thinking this ain't right. There was something terribly wrong with this picture. I got to thinking about all this. That is like demanding my eight-year-old son to figure out calculus or algebra when he is only in the third grade. He can't physically do something he is not developed for.

Then how can God put something in the Bible that black sisters can't physically do? It seems like a contradiction. Ready for the answer? The answer is; he wouldn't, and he didn't. Then why can't black sisters supposedly grow hair like the rest of the women? That is such a sensitive question. Ouch! Perhaps you've wondered the same.

Many claim that they never cut their hair since they came into the truth of Jesus Name baptism and being filled with the Holy

Ghost. And I believe them. But then why is there a difference? Why *can* some new converts grow out their frazzled hair when others *can not*? Why do some sisters relent to cover their short hair with a wig? Or why does it grow to the shoulders then stop all of a sudden? Why do some Apostolic African American sisters give in and get extensions? Why are some sisters feeling such shame towards their hair? Why do they repeatedly feel that their hair is "ugly"? And why does the very mention of all these questions still hurt?

These very pointed questions are not to bring humiliation on anyone. In order to shed light, one must ask. I feel God led me on a journey to find out some answers. One sister e-mailed me and noted that addressing some hair issues could be "an attempt to mock another race." I'm not trying to *mock* anyone or trying to be a separatist here. I'm trying to figure out why there are discrepancies. And why aren't we talking openly about it.

From the onset, it must be said, *there is no difference in people*. Perhaps culturally, but we are all the human race. God Almighty created one race and many nations. There are not many races. Sin conjured up that notion. There are two kinds of people the Bible refers to: the ***saved*** and the ***unsaved.*** God's people and people who don't belong to Him. The Bible says that we are *all* one blood. "***And hath made of one blood all nations of men for to dwell on all the face of the earth***" (Acts 17:26). We are all one body, the saved, sanctified, body of Christ!

No human is different in value from the other. If I took a knife and cut someone from the city of Casma, Hong Kong, or whatever and cut someone else from the village of Ladysmith, Tongo, or whatever, both would bleed red.

My neighbor, a surgeon, Dr. Carolyn Drake, returned

from a trip to Africa. I asked her if there is a difference between black and white. She said that when she cuts into a white person and cuts into a black person, inside they're the same! Ah hah…I knew it. Both have souls and both are going to live in eternity somewhere. Both have need of a Savior, Jesus Christ.

Skin is only the tabernacle that houses the soul. It is sin that wants to label, slice and separate. It's sin that drove Cain to kill his brother. That same sin runs rampant today upon the earth to sever the value of human beings.

When we were new converts we learned in our Bible study lessons that there are three people groups. These groups came from the people who descended from Noah's ark. Ham, Shem and Japeth. So generally speaking, there are three **people groups** *(not races, I'm not playing semantics here, but explaining we all came out of the ark):* Asian, African, and European. We will discuss the mixing of these people groups which eventually caused the genes to determine hair length and texture in each individual. For now, let's start at where it all began by going back to the Garden of Eden.

Introduction

My hope for my children must be that they
respond to the still, small voice of God in their own hearts.

—Andrew Young (1932-)
Quotes from Famous Black Americans

Chapter 1

Back to the Garden

Let's begin were it all started. The Garden of Eden was the place were God created the first man, Adam. The Bible states that Adam was created in the image of God. It also says that God said that it wasn't good for Adam to be alone so He created woman. She was to be a helpmeet for him. In the original Hebrew text it says, "a fitting helper for him". And thus, God created Eve out of the rib of Adam and in the garden the two of them dwelt.

Later in the New Testament, Paul the Apostle uses the same creation account as it relates to Christian ordinances. In Genesis we are told that God established a divine order for authority (Genesis 1:26-31). Paul uses this same principle as he sets up certain regulations for men and women in public worship services. This very axiom of one's outer appearance was established first in the early church. It mattered how a person looked as they entered into the presence of God in a general assembly.

Even before the partaking of the Lord's Supper, Paul deals with the individual as "the Temple of God" which is found in chapter three of the same book (1 Corinthians 3). He then lays out the rules of conduct to sustain decency and order in worship. Their worship was to be in a godly manner not like the all too familiar pagan chaos. This was because the Lord God was not the author of confusion but of peace, as it should be in all churches (I Corinthians 14:33).

Once this fundamental rule was laid down, he continued in the following chapters of the book of first Corinthians chapters 12-15 to deal with what goes on in the church services (i.e. spiritual gifts, distribution of spiritual gifts, characteristics of love, and the order of tongues). He was trying to dispel the divisions and heresies commonly known in Corinth. Paul's teachings of divine order will help us grasp the meaning of the following passages of scriptures. This understanding of a woman's glory will support the foundation that is the fundamental principle of this tributary pursuit, *Her Ebony Glory*. The scriptures read as follows:

First Corinthians, chapter 11:3-16,

1Cor 11:3 But I would have you know, that the head of every man is Christ; and the head of the woman is the man; and the head of Christ is God.
1Cor 11:4 Every man praying or prophesying, having his head covered, dishonoureth his head.
1Cor 11:5 But every woman that prayeth or prophesieth with her head uncovered dishonoureth her head: for that is even all one as if she were shaven.
1Cor 11:6 For if the woman be not covered, let her also be shorn: but if it be a shame for a woman to be shorn or shaven, let her be covered.
1Cor 11:7 For a man indeed ought not to cover his head, forasmuch as he is the image and glory of God: but the woman is the glory of the man.
1Cor 11:8 For the man is not of the woman: but the woman of the man.
1Cor 11:9 Neither was the man created for the woman; but the woman for the man.
1Cor 11:10 For this cause ought the woman to have power on her head because of the angels.

1Cor 11:11 Nevertheless neither is the man without the woman, neither the woman without the man, in the Lord.
1Cor 11:12 For as the woman is of the man, even so 1is the man also by the woman; but all things of God.
1Cor 11:13 Judge in yourselves: is it comely that a woman pray unto God uncovered?
1Cor 11:14 Doth not even nature itself teach you, that, if a man have long hair, it is a shame unto him?
1Cor 11:15 But if a woman have long hair, it is a glory to her: for her hair is given her for a covering.
1Cor 11:16 But if any man seem to be contentious, we have no such custom, neither the churches of God.

This section of scripture deals with how male and female persons should look (outer appearance) as we enter into the presence of God. Quite frankly, they should look distinctively different from each other. The appearance of Christian men and the appearance of Christian women were to be noticeably different. Why did God make a differentiation between the sexes?

The answer is found in verse three of our text. It sets the precedence for this rule: *"the head of every man is Christ; and the head of the woman is the man; and the head of Christ is God."* This tells you the line of authority and the order in which the human species was created. The order goes, God, Christ, the man and then the woman.

I'd like to point out here as a side note, that the head of every man is Christ but the head of *"the"* woman is *the* man, which is her husband only. Many men *(and perhaps women)* like to interpret this verse to say that *all* men are over *every* woman just like Christ is over every man. However this teaching is erroneous. Every man is not the head over every woman. The Amplified version renders it as ***"But I want you to know and***

realize that Christ is the Head of every man, the head of a woman is her husband, and the Head of Christ is God."

This teaching has been passed down unchallenged through the years. Verse three of 1st Corinthians chapter 11 deals primarily with a married couple and their relationship with each other. Thus, the scripture DOES NOT read like this:

The head of every man is Christ;
and the head of every woman is every man.

Let's read it again and understand what it truly says, "... ***the head of every man is Christ; and the head of the woman*** *[singular]* ***is the man*** *[singular]* ***and the head of Christ is God"*** *(1 Cor. 11:3).* Thank the Lord... 'cause I can only submit to one husband at a time.

Incidentally, in Jewish tradition, they believe that married men and married women need to wear a head covering to remind them that there is a Higher Being (God) to be accountable to. And they also believe because "women are on a higher spiritual level than men," women don't need a reminder as much. Consequently, unmarried women and girls do not wear head coverings! This proves the point that Paul was only addressing *married* women.[1] (More about the history of head coverings [veils] in chapter 12).

That was free, now let's move on.

You may ask how does this New Testament passage relate to the creation process in Genesis? It's quite simple. First of all we must realize that God looks at us when we enter into His presence, ***"God looked down from heaven upon the***

children of men" (Psalms 53:2). When a man stands there in God's presence, he only should reflect the image of God as he was created in God's image (Genesis 1:26-27). The only God we humans ever saw was the man, Christ Jesus.

Some say that it speaks differently. It says *they* (man and woman) were made in *his* image. A closer look at that scripture will reveal its meaning. Genesis 1:27 says, ***"So God created man in his own image, in the image of God created he him; male and female created he them."*** The translators could of put the punctuation marks any place. The "male and female" here is referring to all creatures. God made male and female creatures for the sake of procreation (Gen. 1:28).

Woman was not made at this time. She was later pulled from the side of Adam (Gen. 2: 21). Perhaps this is why Adam said, ***"This is now bone of my bones, and flesh of my flesh: she shall be called Woman, because she was taken out of Man "*** (Gen. 2:23).

So to say she was made in God's image is not correct. The two of them together are called "Adam". Another way of saying this is they are "human beings." Better yet, the male and female refer to all of mankind in general. As it takes one male and one female to reproduce its own kind.

Genesis 5: 1-2 reiterates, ***"...In the day that God created man, in the likeness of God made he him; Male and female created he them; and blessed them, and called their name Adam, in the day when they were created."*** By reading this scripture you can see that there is no mention of Eve being created in God's image. The image referred to the physique of the soon coming Messiah, Jesus Christ (2 Cor. 4:4).

By studying the creation account in Genesis we learn that men should not cover their head because he was created in God's image (I Corinthians 11: 4 & 7). He has a right to enter the presence of God uncovered. The woman, on the other hand, was not created in God's image but she reflects the glory of the man so she *should* be covered (verse 5 & 6).

In his article, *"Slipping Past the Harbor: A Study of Biblical Standards Regarding Hair and the Order of Creation,"* Rev. Marvin Treece states that we need to be properly covered. Treece notes "if you do not have the appropriate covering or keeping of one's head (hair), further dealing with God will be on an improper being that he or she is ill equipped to be in the presence of God."[2] When we enter into the presence of God we need to be attired correctly.

Men are allowed to be uncovered in the presence of God because they were made in God's image. When God looks down on man He virtually looks at Himself. When God looks at a woman, he doesn't see His image or form; thus, she should have a covering. She came out of man but both were made out of God. If she has her hair cut like a man, then she removes herself from the distinct order of creation.[3]

In other words, a woman's head must be covered to show her submission to her husband. What if she doesn't have a husband? Well, that's easy, God is her husband. Isaiah 54: 5, ***"For thy Maker is thine husband; the LORD of hosts is his name; and thy Redeemer the Holy One of Israel; The God of the whole earth shall he be called."*** Because of her position at creation (being created secondly or taken out of man) it is uncomely, unseemly, not fitting for a woman to pray with her head uncovered (vs. 13). It's a glory to her to have her head covered.[4]

What is the woman's proper covering, a hat, veil or turban? Her God-given covering is her <u>long hair</u>. The scripture is very direct concerning this. First Corinthians 11:15 says, ***"...for her hair is given her for a covering."*** I'm glad that Paul was plain about this. There should be no question as to what this means. Her hair is a God-given covering not a hat or veil which is man-made. However, there is some confusion about whether a woman should wear a veil or a secondary covering but we will address that subject and its origins in depth in chapter 12.

Long hair on a woman is a symbol of her authority to enter in the presence of God properly. Verse ten of first Corinthians 11 says ***"For this cause ought the woman to have power on her head because of the angels.*** " What kind of power are we taking about here?

The word "power" comes from the Greek word "exousia" that is defined as <u>authority, jurisdiction, liberty, privilege; force; capacity</u> (Strong's Concordance #1849). We find a similar scripture in Luke 10:19 that also uses the same word "power," ***"Behold, I give unto you POWER*** *(emphasis mine)* ***to tread on serpents and scorpions, and over all the power of the enemy: and nothing shall by any means hurt you."***

Although the word "power" is used twice in Luke 10:19, there are two different words used in the original Greek. The Scripture is better rendered "...behold I give unto you AUTHORITY, or behold I give unto you the JURISDICTION or CAPACITY to tread on serpents and scorpions." Any of the definitions above could be inserted.

The "power of the enemy" simply means the force or miraculous power by which he (the devil) manifests his wickedness. In speaking about "serpents and scorpions," Jesus is talking about the power of the devil--demons, evil spirits, and all his cohorts. Hence, we need to bear in mind those Holy Ghost-filled women have authority over the devil and all his entourage!

Of course, God Himself is the ultimate power behind our authority.

Another scriptural example of power distribution is mentioned in Matthew 10:1, ***"...He gave them POWER*** (emphasis mine) ***against unclean spirits, to cast them out, and to heal all manner of sickness and all manner of disease."*** Jesus gave his disciples the authority to act in his behalf.

Here is an illustration of the power of authority. Police officers who direct traffic during rush hour just raise their hand to stop the cars. Do these officers have the *physical* power to stop vehicles if a driver chooses not to stop? No. The police instead use their authority. This was vested in their badge worn on their chest. The government they serve granted it to them.

The same is for our women who obey God's word. Does she have the physical power to stop the forces from raging against her? No. But when she prays or prophesy with her proper covering (uncut hair) she has the authority to put a stop to the devil's devices. God gives her supernatural power and will back her up. Isaiah 58:8 says, ***"...the glory of the Lord shall be thy rereward,"*** meaning 'rear guard' or 'he'll watch your back'. Her obedience (deminstrated by her actions) gives her such authority.

When we follow the plan of God by submitting to the man in our life (husband) we show we honor God. Allowing him to be the head of the home shows that we are willing to come under authority. We in turn obtain spiritual authority. We become the glory of our husband, as stated in the previous verses.

When we line up to God's word willingly, we naturally invite the glory of God in our life. It's his glory that will watch over you. By being obedient you will receive all of God's power, provision and protection.

You are not exempt just because you don't have a husband here on earth. The scripture clearly states that the Lord is your husband (Isa 54:5). This goes for all women, young and old who are not *yet* married also.

Let's examine the word "because" in our scripture study. ***"For this cause ought the woman to have power on her head because of the angels"*** *(verse 10).* The word *because* means 'denoting the channel of an act; through.' I heard an awesome illustration by Sister Linda Reed on her CD-ROM, *Guardians of His Glory*.

She stated that the angels are channeling a holy woman's power through her. Just as a nanny is given a charge to watch over a young toddler's safety, so is the angels of the Almighty given charge to watch over our safety.[5] (Psalms 91:11 clearly states this promise).

And yes, there are those other denominations that receive the Holy Ghost. How about them you might ask? Their women all have cut hair and they get the Holy Ghost. True, when you go to their conferences they have the worship, the great song services and the demonstrations of jubilation and such. They too, like to feel the presence of the Lord.

Sister Reed explains that in their services you can feel the grace of God, and the presence of God in a measure, but they don't have the glorious visitations like people who walk in holiness. We have the fullness of truth. Yet these denominations don't have the level of glory that we have.[6]

Howbeit, God is probably trying to lead them. They don't worship God in spirit and *truth*. They have not provided a place holy, as it were, unto the Lord for him to dwell in.[7]

There is a noticeable difference, whereas when you go to a holiness conference, people worship in the fullness of truth. You can feel the Shekinah glory of God. You hear people say, "we felt the glory cloud tonight." Feeling the presence of God in a powerful way is awesome. I'm glad we have this privilege.

For a more in-depth look at the spiritual, historical, and etheric significance of hair I strongly recommend my book, My Hair, My Glory". There are over 300 works cited (footnotes) on the significance of long hair. I know you'll enjoy reading it!

Now, let's move on to examine what the meaning of "long" is. ***"But if a woman have long hair, it is a glory to her: for her hair is given her for a covering" (1Cor 11:15).*** What does it mean to have "**long**" hair? The Greek word "komao" is simply defined as "**to wear tresses of hair**." A "**tress**" according to Merriam Webster dictionary is a **long lock [strand or ringlet] of hair**.

According to Thayer's Greek-English Lexicon of the New Testament, **long** means, "**to let the hair grow, or have long hair**." The Apostle uses the word "komao" in the verb tense. A verb is the part of speech that expresses action or to be doing something. Thus, **let it grow** means *don't stop it from growing.*

One definition I heard for the word long was "**should continue having long hair**". For example a man interrupts the growth of his hair by going to the barber while a Christian woman leaves hers long and uninterrupted.[8]

The Strong's Concordance says it more properly, that we should "**provide for**," that is, by implying, "**to carry off [things] that 'as if to harm' [our hair]**." In plain English this means *don't do stuff to your hair that is harmful and causes it to stop the growth.* Abusive hair care has kept some women from growing long hair. This very topic is studied in depth in chapter

eleven.

For a woman to have long uncut hair shows the world a sign of her submission to authority. Obedience to God's Word, the ultimate authority, shows that a woman is in true submission. Loretta and David Bernard say in their book, *In Search of Holiness,* "nature teaches her to have long hair as opposed to shorn hair (cut hair) or a shaven head. It is one of God's methods for maintaining a distinction between male and female."[9] If she wears her covering (long hair) she has the privilege to pray, prophesy, preach, and testify as the Lord leads without being ashamed.

The words ashamed and shame describe the emotional feeling brought on by sin. The American Heritage dictionary says it is "a painful emotion caused by a strong sense of guilt, embarrassment, unworthiness, or disgrace." The Bible says it is a shame for a woman to pray or to prophesy with an uncovered head. If she cuts her hair it is the same as being completely shaven (1 Corinthians 11: 6).

Thus, if a woman who is saved, that is, filled with the Holy Ghost, baptized in Jesus Name, understands this principle she will not want to do anything against God's Word so that she may draw close to Him. She'll want to do what is pleasing to the Lord, ***"...if ye love me, keep my commandments "*** (John 14:15).

Once she prays through and is taught this concept then she is responsible to allow her hair to grow out and not hinder it from doing so. She must do all she can to help her hair grow out to the length God intends it to be. The Apostle Paul in the book of Corinthians teaches this principle. We can grasp the clearer meaning when we understand the concept of the order of creation in the Garden of Eden at the beginning of time.

[1] Rabbi N. Silberberg, *AskMoses.com*

[2] "Slipping Past the Harbor: A Study of Biblical Standards Regarding Hair and the Order of Creation", Reverend Marvin Treece, article taken from:

www.altupc.com/articles/harbor.htm, p 2.

[3] Ibid, p3.

[4] Elizabeth Rice Handford, *Your Clothes Say it For You*, (Murfreesboro, TN: Sword of the Lord Publishers, 1976) p59.

[5] Linda Reed, Guardians of His Glory, CD-Rom

[6] Ibid.

[7] Ibid.

[8] Juli Jasinski, *Daring Dos*, p8-9.

[9] Loretta Bernard and David Bernard, *In Search of Holiness*, (Hazelwood, MO: Word Aflame Press, 1981) p124-125.

I feel that the human mind

has not achieved anything greater than the ability to share feelings and thoughts through language.

—James Earl Jones (1931-)

Quotes from Famous Black Americans

Chapter 2

A Balm in Gilead

"Is there not a balm in Gilead?" was my friend's response as I spoke to her on the phone. She, a woman of God and a pastor's wife, was moved as I unloaded my burden concerning our sisters of color and the hair scripture. This sister knew all to well about the struggle of black women and their hair.

Talking to her was like talking to God face to face. Those that know her personally know she walks close with the Lord. We talked awhile and cried a bit then we prayed. We got off the phone refreshed. Yet, the questions still filled my mind and the dilemma still remained unresolved.

She prayed that the Lord would lead and guide me in my research on this subject. She asked the Lord that he would put the right people in my way to enlighten my path. That he did. She knew that it would take more than just one woman to explain the situation and its complexities. How could she express in a few words what she's known about all her life?

Her response lead me to believe that God was going to bring healing to our sisters of color. Perhaps there will be an interracial healing as well. I later learned that this hair issue for African-Americans and all ladies of color (those from other countries as well) is so intertwined with racial issues. I hate to say I didn't really know that these issues existed.

One brother chewed me out because I didn't know anything about black issues. He said it was "white willful ignorance." I told him to hold it, back up and take a breath because it was quite the contrary. How can I care about something that I'm not aware of? History records that America did not believe what was going on in Germany during World War II until they were made aware of it. They needed to see photographs as proof of the gas chambers. Then they went in and did something about it. That is why Hitler got away with killing so many Jews. The world wasn't cognizant of such a deplorable tragedy. When they were made aware, they took action.

On the same note, I couldn't be held responsible for something I didn't know about. If you weren't brought up knowing there is a problem then whose fault can that be? We can't assume people know about issues. I let this brother know that growing up in my family, in the city of Santa Clara, California we never discussed "race." My father was an immigrant from Holland and an unbeliever to boot. He hated the ways of Americans. My parents usually fought over other things like religious issues. Americans in general, white or black, we're all a thorn in my dad's side.

Here is what Jim Yohe said about racism as a whole in his book, *Confronting Racism: Putting God's Grace over Race*, "There is no magic wand that the church or the government can wave that will make all things equal. There are a great variety of economic disparities within the white race itself. Real change will only occur when individuals are willing to risk striking up personal friendships with people of other races with the underlying goal of honest communication."[1]

Yohe continues, "In America, the majority of whites may give lip service to the need for racial equality, but actually most whites feel that they have done all they can do."[2] Yohe has a great deal to say about racism in his book. He is convinced it can be resolved in the church but only on an individual level.

According to Stephen Strang, founding editor of

Charisma Magazine, says in his article, Let's Join Fred Price's Crusade, "The church must take a leadership role in racial reconciliation by dealing first with its own racism."[3] He suggests the church leaders should join with those in identifying the seriousness of this problem and focusing on solutions.

My rebuttal is how can people take a leadership role and do all that they can do if they don't realize there is first a problem? It's not willful ignorance; it's lack of knowledge and understanding. We perhaps need to hear more of an outcry of the black communities and their experienced discrepancies.

I found one of the biggest justifications for racial discrimination that in modern times is the held belief in evolution. This is what inspired Hitler in his quest to establish a "master race."[4] So how does all this tie in with the hair issue and the black woman? Girls of *no* color cannot empathize so such because they never walked in the shoes of girls with color. They are not aware of the issues that surround a black person. I was blind to the dilemma myself.

I'm glad God dealt with me to write on the subject. Shakespeare once said, "the pen is mightier than the sword." I just hope opening this Pandora's box will at the very least get people to be moved to action. Somebody needs to say something. I know by talking with many Apostolic ladies that they are interested in knowing and understanding what the sisters of color are feeling.

No doubt there is a myriad of feelings about this subject of hair. The issue may seem so complicated that there is no answer. Some just want to ignore it. Some say there is no difference, no struggle, no problem, just leave the subject alone. Others want me to reach out and talk about it. And others may think it isn't any of my business. Ironically, God has something to say about it. He has been faithful to send me a few ladies who have encouraged me from day one to get on with it and get the book written.

Evangelist Carlton Clark said to me one time that attempting to understand the Black culture in America is to enter a labyrinth that I may not soon emerge from. This may be true and I'm happy to do so. We can pin point some very definite historical details to shed some light on this evolving predicament.

When my friend cried out "is there not a balm in Gilead," I didn't know what to answer her. I don't know, is there a balm to heal the hurting wound? Is there anything out there for them? The scripture says, ***"Is there no balm in Gilead; is there no physician there? Why then is not the health of the daughter of my people recovered?"*** (Jeremiah 8:22). That is a good question, Jeremiah!

If there *is* a balm in Gilead and a physician is there then why is not the health of the daughter of God's people not recovered? This paradoxical question by Jeremiah to Israel is closely paralleled to the black enigma. We can say that the Lord is the healing balm and the church today has the ability like physicians to apply the ointment to the wounded. The next question is why are so many ladies not recovering.

I believe women from all over the country can receive a healing as need be. Many have already overcome the obstacles of prejudice and discrimination caused by racism. Some however, may continue to feel a sharp sting at the very mention of how this religious bigotry can still exist today. This is how Jeremiah must of felt. Perhaps he thought how could Israel, which produced a healing balm, still be wounded herself? Why can't she apply her own ointment on her own wound and be healed?

The healing balm came from trees grown in the rough mountainous area in the Middle East. How ironic that the soothing ointment was produced in the rough area of modern

Jordan. The inhabitants were none other than the rugged tribes of Reuben and Gad. It's amazing how anything could exist there. The roughest terrain grew the balsam tree that flourished in such a harsh climate.

Sometimes in our life the hardest times and most difficult things (trials) bring about the most healing. A rabbi once said that no one really has a whole heart until first it is broken. When the circumstances seem harsh and unbearable, and our hearts are broken, it's there we come across sources of strength and healing that defy explanation.

The fragrant glutinous sap was extracted by means of repeated lacerations. The gum was quickly released through these incisions caused by an axe or spear. The substance was sometimes made into incense. And also had valuable medicinal purposes. When the jabs of prejudge stab you it is then that Jesus releases the healing flow of the Holy Ghost through your soul. The sweet fragrance of His presence comes so near as we draw closer to His side.

The book of Psalms 46:1 says, ***"God is our refuge and strength, a very present help in trouble."***This region was well known for this healing balm and their physicians who knew how to administer it. Phoenicia and Egypt were great recipients of medication. The church is well known for the healing virtue of Jesus Christ. Others come from afar off to gather it in their souls. Take a moment and thank Him for that healing flow. ***"He healeth the broken in heart, and bindeth up their wounds"*** (Psalms 147:3). What a great promise we have in Christ. Yes, there **is** a Balm in Gilead.

[1] Jim Yohe, Confronting Racism, (Indianapolis, IN: Faithchild Publishing) 2000, p31.
[2] ibid, p30.
[3] Stephen Strang, "Let's Join Fred Price's Crusade," *Charisma Magazine*, April 1998, p122.
[4] www.ChristianAnswers.Net, "What are the Consequences of False Beliefs about the Origin of Races?" Eden Communications, 2002.

> *Author's Note: This is a great web site with many articles pertinent to the racial issues, human origins, and Christianity. Check them out!*

Success is to be measured not so
much by the position that one has reached in life
as by the obstacles which he has over come
while trying to succeed.

—Booker T. Washington (1856-1915)
Quotes from Famous Black Americans

Chapter 3

Epoch of Nations

When Noah and his family came out of the ark, survivors of the great flood, they were told by God to replenish the earth. In fulfilling this command, the human race was to spread and repopulate the face of the earth. Instead of complete obedience they located in one specific area. The group grew large enough to build a city with a tower that was used as a center of humanity. The Lord, however, was not pleased.

The action of the people resulted in a judgement by God. He changed their language so that they could not understand one another. In their confusion they scattered. God stopped this defiant society from continuing their sin. And thus, the beginning of nations came out of this dispersion.

The Bible records that Noah's three sons Shem, Ham, and Japheth were scattered throughout the region. The descendants of Shem settled in Assyria, Syria, Persia, northern Arabia, and Mesopotamia. And his two brothers lived elsewhere with their family clans.

The sons of Ham were Cush, Mizraim, Phut, and Canaan. Some of the nations to spring out of this people group were the Ethiopians, Egyptians, Libyans, and Canaanites. They settled in Africa and Arabia. The last son of Noah, Japheth settled in Asia Minor, Caucasia, and Europe. From them came the Israelites, Russians, Germans, Britons, Scythians, and many others.

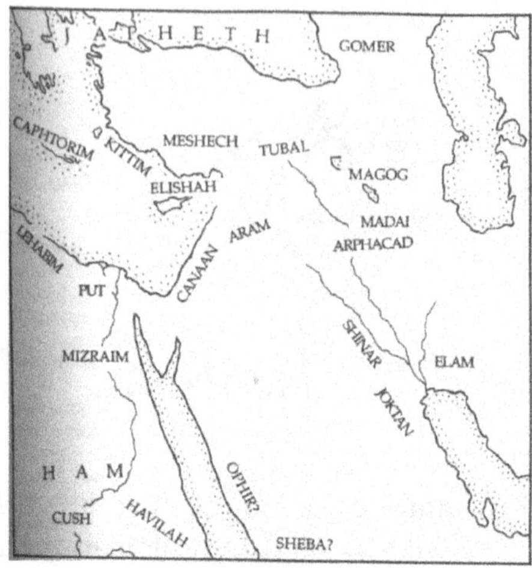

Identity of peoples
OF JAPHETH
Gomer = Cimmerians
Madai = Medes
Javan = Greeks
Ashkenaz = Scythians
Elishah = Crete
Tarshish = W. Spain
Kittim = Cyprus

OF HAM
Cush = Ethiopia
Mizraim = Egypt
Lehabites = Lybians
Caphtorim = Cretans
Hittites, etc. = Pre-Israelite inhabitants of Canaan

OF SHEM (SEMITES)
Eber = Hebrews
Aram = Syrians
(in third millennium, north: in second, next to Canaan)
Arphaxad = N. Iraq?

Table of Nations (Map 1)

Over a period of time people began to intermarry and generate certain societal institutions distinct to each region. As people started to adapt to the climate, their human bodies began to develop features that aided in survival and proliferation of the human race. Migrations from draughts and famines played a part in causing new genetic combinations. Also, when wars were fought, captives were often brought back, enslaved and inbred.

Thus human beings physically adapted to their climate over hundreds of years. The skeletal structure, muscle size, height, hair texture, nose shape, eye shape and color, lip shape, and pigmentation of skin all evolved through these aforementioned reasons over a period of time.[1]

The darkest skin colors were concentrated along the equator were it is generally the hottest. Their skin naturally darkened in the hot sun. *Ever get sunburned then that it turned into a tan color during the summer?* The lightest of skin colors are found far north where the temperatures are extremely frigid. The small amount of sunlight that falls upon northwest Europe explains why skin is so light or appears to be form of de-pigmentation.

Skin pigmentation is made up of carotene and melanin. Heavy pigmentation in the tropics or the Torrid Zone act as a buffer from ultraviolet rays to prevent overproduction of vitamin D. The people groups who live in hotter climates and have moderate brown skin are in a proper balance for the environments in which they live.[2]

"If you have a great deal of melanin, and live in a country where there is little sunshine" says ChristianAnswers.Net, in their article, *Where did the Human Races come from,* "it will be harder for you to get enough vitamin D (which needs sunshine for its production in your body)." They continue, "you may suffer from vitamin D deficiency, which could cause a bone disorder such as rickets."[3]

Some have an erroneous notion that skin color was some curse put on the descendents of Ham. God has never cursed anyone with "blackness" or darkness of skin. If there was a curse where skin color was involved, the curse always turned them white.[4] For example, Miriam, the sister of Moses was struck with leprosy and her skin turned "white as snow" (Numbers 12:1-10). Elisha's servant, Gehazi was also struck with this malady in 2 Kings 1-17.

It's hard to fit everyone into one mold so genealogists have done their best to classify people into three fundamental people groups, Negroid, Mongoloid, Caucasoid. They base their categories on skin color, hair texture, eye shape, nose shape, and lip shape. With today's fast-paced, ever roving transient society these classifications are inadequate. In spite of whatever classifications or systematic groupings there may be, these terms are no longer in scientific use.

This information is useful when studying the origin of hair. Hair texture is believed to have undergone a gradual change as humans adapted to their climate. Hair gets its color from a pigment called melanin and is responsible for all the colors of hair from yellow to black.[5]

It's interesting to note, over a period of years that in colder climates where the sunshine is less intense, the color of hair grew lighter. The eyes were even a much lighter color. Cold air produced thinner noses, to prevent nostrils from inhaling too much cold air. Arms and legs of people tend to be shorter in order to reduce heat loss through radiation.

The hair of people in cooler climates grows fast and the extreme cold makes the hair straight. On the other hand, under conditions of extreme heat, wooly hair found common to many African people, provided insulation for the top of the head and protected the brain from injury. Wider noses allowed hotter air to be cooled when inhaled. Long, thin bodies provided the body's surface to perspire and evaporate perspiration as a means of cooling the body's temperature.[6]

Natural geographic boundaries such as mountains, deserts, forest, large bodies of water and the like, caused people to reproduce certain genetic traits among people living within that geographic area. In today's population we can find a variation of physical traits and features on just about every continent. The epoch of nations can trace its origin to the dispersion of the descendents of Shem, Ham, and Japheth. Now, let's take a look at God's idea of beauty.

[1] Latif, Sultan A. & Naimah, "Black Beauty Standards," *Slavery: The African American Psychic Trauma,* (Communications Group, Inc, 1999) p225.
[2] Ibid p226.
[3] WWW.ChristianAnswers.Net *"Where Did the Human Race Come From?"* Eden Communications, 2002.

Author's Note: This is a great web site with many articles pertinent to racial issues and Christianity. Check them out!

[4] Wayne Perryman, "The 1993 Trial on the Curse of Ham," *The African Culture Heritage Topical Bible*, (Pneuma Life Publishing, Bakersfield, CA 1995) p39-40.
[5] "Human Hair Growth," Grolier Multimedia Encyclopedia CD-ROM.
6 Latif, Sultan A. & Naimah, "Black Beauty Standards," *Slavery: The African American Psychic Trauma,* (Communications Group, Inc, 1999) p226.

PICTURE CREDITS
Map 1—Lawrence O. Richards, *The Bible Reader's Companion,* (Chariot Victor Publishing, Wheaton, IL, 1991) p31.

What happens to a dream deferred?

Does it dry up like a raisin in the sun?

—Langston Hughes (1902-1967)

Quotes from Famous Black Americans

Chapter 4

God's Idea of Beauty

King David one time cried out in Psalms ninety verse seventeen, ***"And let the beauty of the LORD our God be upon us and establish thou the work of our hands upon us."*** This was one of the many cries of the king's heart in that day. This too has been the cry of my heart. But just what is the "beauty of the Lord?" The beauty of the Lord is when He grants us his approval on our lives. His glory shines down on us. The favor of the Lord just seems to radiate through our lives. He establishes our work through his grace as we endeavor to please Him. To walk with God knowing we have His regard makes life worth the living. David, the king of Israel found that place of friendship with God.

David's desire was to have the beauty of God reigning down on his life. He knew God would establish his works with good results. He wanted Israel placed securely in a position so the surrounding nations would know that Jehovah is the One True God. When God's approval is upon someone, it seems that their godly works and endeavors generate beautiful results.

The Bible also states that, ***"the LORD taketh pleasure in his people: he will beautify the meek with salvation"*** (Psalms 149:4). Salvation is comely upon the once-lost sinner. The Almighty makes everything new in the life of the believer. His beauty rays begin shining down on the life of the individual. He leads the newborn Christian into a deep relationship with Himself.

The Bible also states that ***"the LORD taketh pleasure in his people: he will beautify the meek with salvation"*** (Psalms 149:4). Salvation is comely upon the once-lost sinner. The Almighty makes everything new in the life of the believer. His beauty rays begin shining down on the life of the individual. He leads the newborn Christian into a deep relationship with Himself.

Jesus made it quite clear however, that we would have an enemy whom wishes to snuff out any goodness from God. Hatred is the devil's most powerful weapon. He uses it to defeat the purpose and plan of God. The driving force behind his cunning deceit is his contempt for God's word.

Contrary to God's standard of beauty, the devil has devised his own beauty ideal which is not of God. His is one of lust, malice and greed. The devil's standard of beauty is made up so that people strain themselves trying to conform futilely to an ultimate form of physical perfection. The beauty of God comes from above and is not man-made. The devil's standard of beauty, on the other hand, was belched out of hell and has caused many to suffer the misery of jealousy, competition and strife.

God is nowhere near this worldly realm. The word of God teaches us to guard ourselves against this trap. Peter, the Apostle quotes one of the most pre-eminent scripture in the Bible, ***"But as he which hath called you is holy, so be ye holy in all manner of conversation*** [behavior] ***because it is written, Be ye holy; for I am holy"*** (1 Peter 1:15-16).

As the ancient nation of Egypt was prospering, God told his people, Israel to separate themselves from their evil ways. He told them to come out of that country and be a holy separate people. The last three books of the law (Leviticus, Numbers, and Deuteronomy) dealt with important principles needed to be adhere to. They had to carry out the commands in order to sanctify themselves to the Lord.

The Lord God was clear how the Israelites were to live. Through the sacrifices of animals came their atonement or covering of sins. Well over a hundred times the words "holy" or "holiness" was stated in the Law. The basic idea was so that the Israelites could be consecrated to God and separated from other surrounding nations.

When the word "holy" was applied to God, it denoted his "uniqueness" and "distinctiveness" from everything that was worldly and wrong; when applied to man it denoted that one must live a life of purity and obedience. Once these foundations were established through a series of ceremonial practices, they then made preparation for the entering of Canaan.

This was done as a foreshadowing of the New Testament believer. Thus, atonement and holiness was welded together just as we, the redeemed by the blood of the Lamb are to live a separated and holy life which prepares us to live forever in heaven. The Lord taught the children of Israel to be a clean, separate people. And that didn't change for the New Testament believer!

First Thessalonians 4:4-8 says, ***"That every one of you should know how to possess his vessel in sanctification and honour; Not in the lust of concupiscence, even as the Gentiles which know not God: That no man go beyond and defraud his brother in any matter: because that the Lord is the avenger of all such, as we also have forewarned you and testified. For God hath not called us unto uncleanness, but unto holiness. He therefore that despiseth, despiseth not man, but God, who hath also given unto us his holy Spirit."*** The Holy Ghost teaches us how to posses our body in sanctification that brings the Lord glory. The Lord has not called us to uncleanness but holiness. A separate life is what is required for us to please God.

Paul admonished the New Testament church, ***"Wherefore come out from among them, and be ye separate, saith the Lord, and touch not the unclean thing; and I will receive you, and will be a Father unto you, and ye shall be my sons and daughters, saith the Lord Almighty. Having therefore these promises, dearly beloved, let us cleanse ourselves from all filthiness of the flesh and spirit, perfecting holiness in the fear of God"*** (2 Corinthains 6:17-18, 7:1).

The devil's false beauty standard can never measure up to God's requirement of separation and holiness. We should not get caught up in trying to appease the flesh. Many of us are all-too-aware of the strong pull of the world. Its system tries to allure us to look just like them. The same was required for Israel not to dress like the Egyptians and surrounding nations. In this day and age, the world expects us to copy their ways. And if we don't we are made to feel like a freak.

Some unwary saints of God have been caught up in Satan's trap. Titus two instructs us, ***"For the grace of God that bringeth salvation hath appeared to all men teaching us that, denying ungodliness and worldly lusts, we should live soberly, righteously, and godly, in this present world"*** (Titus 2:11-12).

The beauty of God's grace teaches us to give up ungodly living and worldly passion, and to live a self-controlled, spirit-led, upright life in this world. He rescued us from all wickedness. First Peter 2:9-11 tells us, ***"But ye are a chosen generation, a royal priesthood, an holy nation, a peculiar people; that ye should shew forth the praises of him who hath called you out of darkness into his marvellous light; Which in time past were not a people, but are now the people of God: which had not obtained mercy, but now have obtained mercy. Dearly beloved, I beseech you as strangers and pilgrims, abstain from fleshly***

lusts, which war against the soul." His blood makes us pure to live for Him alone. And by His power we are eager to do so.

Perhaps you've been stung by the devil's beauty standard. I know I was. I remember as girl growing up, if you weren't the cute cheerleader, pompom type, you were dirt. You had to have a perfect voluptuous figure and a smashing smile. Girls got caught up into trying to meet these demands altering as many parts of their anatomy as possible.

Especially in the 70's, I remember the heartthrob of America was Farrah Ferrcett, you know, "Charlie's Angels." Everyone wanted to copy her shaggy feathered haircut. The beauty shops warned women that they just *had* to get their "dead ends" cut off in order to be beautiful. It was a money making scam. I recall being ever so furious. My hair never acted right. I couldn't get it feathered like hers if I wanted to. I could never measure up to their beauty standard. I hated it! All those cutesy chicks on the jiggle TV shows drove me crazy.

As I researched into the history of black woman's hair, I discover her unfortunate plight. She too, has been stung by this predicament. I learned that hair for the black woman has always been troublesome not just in the 60's or 70's but it goes further back in history. Now, let's step back in time and learn were it started.

When I found I had crossed that line,
[on her first escape from slavery, 1845],
I looked at my hands to see if I was the same person. There was such a glory over everything.

—Harriet Tubman (1820-1913-)
Quotes from Famous Black Americans

Chapter 5

God, The Righteous Judge

I found the history of African-American hair to be extremely fascinating. And because the average non-woman-of-color knows little about the black lady's hair, history or haunt, she too, will most likely find this chapter exceptionally interesting. The woman of color's unfortunate plight started when the men and women where ripped from their country and brought to the Americas. They were carried across the vast ocean waters by way of slave trade lasting over 400 years (over six generations).

This portion of research brought some clarity to various questions that were cloudy in my mind. Some of the thought-provoking questions are as follows: Were Africans the only slaves in the history of mankind? When did slavery start anyway? Should the U.S. government issue a formal apology to the descendants of African slaves? Understanding some of these facts helped shed some light for me on this situation.

I ascertained from my first inquiry that Africans were not the first slaves. History records for example that during 5th century B.C, the Golden Age of Greece, their citizens had slaves. The Spartan people had always relied on a vast population of land slaves called *helots*. These slaves provided food by working the fields. Because of the number of slave revolts, the government was forced to develop armies to control them.

This brought about the development of societal classes. Each group had different rights. The rich were at the top and at the bottom were slaves. They were considered the "invisible" portion of ancient society. Although Athens was a democratic society, about one-third of the population were slaves. Some slaves were treated as household servants; others were worked to death in mines.[1]

We also find that in New Testament times, Paul the Apostle referred to slaves. He taught that born-again masters were to treat their slaves with compassion, equity, and refrain from threats knowing they too have a heavenly Master who watches all (Ephesians 6:9, Colossians 4:1).

Paul wrote a letter to his friend Philemon regarding a runaway slave. Onesimus who ran from Philemon ended up providentially in jail with the Apostle Paul. Paul preached to him and he was converted. This slave listened diligently and gave his heart to God. Paul entreated Philemon in his letter to receive him as a brother and not to chastise harshly (Philemon verse 15-18). This passage of scripture indicates a prime example of kindness shown to a slave. God's word was clear in how a person, free or bond, should be treated.

Old Testament Jews were warned against exacting services without payment (Jeremiah 22:13). They were taught in the Law of Moses to be prompt with payment of their wages and to be just in their business affairs with employees. God's people were to treat their servants and slaves with impartiality at all times. Some people may think, as I did, that slavery occurred only once. Perhaps you thought the same thing. I thought that it only happened during 1450 AD to 1870 AD. But as one searches the scriptures we can find that slavery was in existence even during early Bible times.

Joseph's brothers, for instance, sold him to Egypt as a slave. By this one can assume that slavery was in full force and customary during this time in Egypt. Interestingly, the first mention of institutionalized slavery in the Bible is found with Israel's enslavement to Egypt. Prior to this event, God prophesied to Abraham of the impending bondage that his descendants (nation of Israel) would suffer (Genesis 15:13). Later in Bible history, we also read of Israel's continual sin, which leads them into two other captivities, Babylonian 6th and 5th centuries BC and Assyrian 9th century BC.

Their first enslavement begins around 1706 BC with the oppression of Egypt. And it ended for Israel under the reign of Rameses II, the prominent Pharaoh in the book of Exodus. The Bible teaches us that the children of Israel suffered bondage during this time for over 400 years (Genesis 15:13, Acts 7:6). How ironic that the African slave trade and Israel's Egyptian bondage both lasted about 400 years! We'll soon learn that there's an interesting reason for that.

Here is a short history lesson. The monolithic empire of Egypt was in power for 3,000 years. It was a flourishing kingdom and one of the earliest known civilizations. This kingdom was mostly settled along the upper part of the 4,100-mile Nile River. Egypt produced magnificent structures and delicate works of art, some written in hieroglyphic form dating back to 3200 BC. The Hebrew people, during the time of their slavery, built nearly half of all Egypt's temples that have survived the riggers of time and can be viewed to this day.

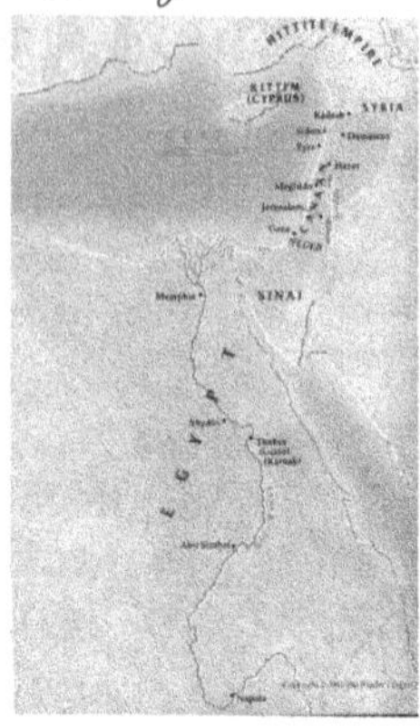

Land of Egypt during the reign of Rameses II: Pharaoh of the Exodus (Map 2)

Most African-Americans claim to be descendants of this great ancient land. You come from a long line of inventors, scientists, writers, and educators. This however, brings us to the third question I mentioned earlier: *Should the U.S. government issue a formal apology to the descendants of African slaves?* I think yes and no. That may sound like I'm undecided but I'm not. I believe an apology for the current racial sting (especially in the church) is appropriate and would indeed mend a world of hurt. And if an official apology is not befitting then steps toward parity should be taken. This could only foster a strong sense of unity and build the love of God in the church and bring about revival.

My hypothesis on the situation is that early Christianity didn't do her job in evangelizing the continent of Africa. Perhaps when the Ethiopian eunuch heard the word of God, was baptized, and went his way rejoicing (Acts 8:39) what did he do when he got home? Did he drop the ball by not telling the plan of salvation to all of Ethiopia? Why didn't Philip do any follow-up on the new convert? Apparently, fifteen hundred miles (i.e. New

York City to Tulsa) was too far for the church to reach a new believer. Just think if there was more of an evangelistic outreach to Ethiopia during the early church, history would have been written differently then how we know it. The Gospel would of spread to all the countries in Africa. Jesus Name saints would have been everywhere.

According to John W. Mbiti, in his book, *Introduction to African Religion* he states "it is believed in Egypt that Christianity was first brought there by Saint Mark in the year 42 AD."[2] Tradition states that Peter sent out John Mark on a mission trip to Egypt. He founded a church in Alexandria (NE of Cairo), of which he became bishop, and suffered martyrdom in the eighth year of Nero.[3]

Supposedly, Christianity spread over northern Africa, as far as present day Morocco. It finally reached into the Nile Valley and Sudan. During the seventh century, history records that the population of these areas was one-third believers in Jesus. We know however, that Christianity itself (One God Truth) was severely watered down by 325AD in the days of Emperor Constantine. The church lost its Holy Ghost power and apostolic influence.

In addition to this unfortunate plight of the dying True Church, a few years after the alleged prophet, Muhammad died (632AD) his ogre followers began to spread into Africa. They came to conquer not with the love of Christ but by the sword of puissance. They swept across Egypt and North Africa within less than a century. Islam established itself wherever the Arabs conquered. The same happened in the Horn of Africa and partly the East Coast of Africa. At the same time it is reported that the Arab Muslims turned Africans into slaves whom they marketed, exported or used in their homes and estates, for more than a thousand years up to the present century. Shockingly, slavery has not yet come to an end for some. It was reported in 1989, that there are Africans enslaved by Arabs in some countries such as the Sudan.[4]

As it deepened its roots across northern Africa and the Sahara, Islam managed to wipe out Christianity partially in some places and completely in others. There remained only a remnant of Christianity (Catholicism) in Egypt, and the faith finally died out completely in Sudan. A church without truth and power can't stand against this abhorrent evil. The result of this is that the entire continent of Africa has become at least one-third Islam dominant. It is interesting to note that of all Christianity that was conquered by Arab Muslims, they never did totally wipe out Christendom in Ethiopia.

As I delve deeper into this topic I found that one black preacher brought out a transversal point about African slavery. He stated very poignantly, that he was glad the ships came to lead the Africans away. He believes that God Almighty loved Africa so much so that He used drastic means to bring her out of a life of sin and darkness. When one considers all the tribal warfare that goes on in Africa and the multiplicity of problems—drought, famine, dissension, political strife—one would be grateful the ships came.

Rev. Earl W. Carter Sr., founder and senior pastor of Christ Ministries Church of God (COGIC) in Orlando, Florida declared that God delivered Africans from idol worship, darkness, and ignorance to bring them into the knowledge of the One True God.[5] He declared that the trouble is not with the white man's oppression but with the great God of the Bible. As shocking as this may be, here is what he had to say.

In his book, *No Apology Necessary, Just Respect,* Rev. Carter Sr., says "we were [once] on top, but now we're not because we picked a fight with God".[6] He holds to the fact that messing with God's children is a serious offense. For ancient Egypt to enslave God's kids meant that God would bring about retribution. Carter brings out some very interesting scriptures to back up his point.

He reasons that "Isaiah 19 speaks about God's judgement of Egypt because of its idolatry, witchcraft and sorcery."[7] It is well known that Africa in general worships idols and pagan gods. Let's read the Isaiah passage:

Isaiah 19:1-5 " The burden of Egypt. Behold, the LORD rideth upon a swift cloud, and shall come into Egypt: and the idols of Egypt shall be moved at his presence, and the heart of Egypt shall melt in the midst of it. And I will <u>set the Egyptians against the Egyptians</u>: <u>and they shall fight every one against his brother, and every one against his neighbour</u>; <u>city against city, and kingdom against kingdom</u>. And the spirit of Egypt shall fail in the midst thereof; and I will destroy the counsel thereof: and they shall seek to the idols, and to the charmers, and to them that have familiar spirits, and to the wizards. And <u>the Egyptians will I give over into the hand of a cruel lord; and a fierce king shall rule over them,</u> saith the Lord, the LORD of hosts. And the waters shall fail from the sea, and the river shall be wasted and dried up."

Carter later drops a bomb of truth on our head. He refers to the scripture in Ezekiel 30:9, ***"In that day shall messengers go forth from me in <u>ships</u> to make the careless Ethiopians afraid, and great pain shall come upon them, as in the day of Egypt: for, lo, it cometh."*** He explains that "it was the Lord" who sent the ships to carry the Africans away. God had a divine plan in mind.

"He raised up the white man," Carter continues "to bring the ships to pick us up and enslave us." "The reason the white man can't stand us," he explains "is because of what it says in Ezekiel 32:9." Here is the scripture; ***"I will also vex the hearts of <u>many people</u>, when I shall bring thy destruction among the***

nations, into the countries which thou hast not known." Carter firmly believes that it was God who caused the heart of the white man to be vexed against the blacks.[8] Hatred not only comes from the *white* man but also from "***many people***" of various colors.

I want to interject here that while this may be true it doesn't justify *hate* and *prejudge*, but rather *explains* why it exists. Jesus taught his New Testament Church to *"**love one another,**"* (John 13:34). The Apostle John reiterates the Lord's words by saying, "***We know that we have passed from death unto life, because we love the brethren. He that loveth not his brother abideth in death. Whosoever hateth his brother is a murderer: and ye know that no murderer hath eternal life abiding in him***" (1John 3:14-15). "***If a man say, I love God, and hateth his brother, he is a liar: for he that loveth not his brother whom he hath seen, how can he love God whom he hath not seen?"*** (1 John 4:20).

These scriptures teach *love* [benevolence] not *hate*. ***"A new commandment I give unto you, that ye love one another; as I have loved you, that ye also love one another"*** (John 13:34). And that is written as plain as the nose on my face! The Gospel of Jesus Christ was love, and love was the fulfilling [completion] of the law (Romans 13:10). Of the three things that dwell in the believer, first Corinthians 13:13 says, *love* is the greatest.

How else will the world know we are His disciples? The answer is in John 13:35; we are to have love one to another. The Lord's teaching of this principle was very timely knowing that His newly born church would have to confront this evil.

The apostle Peter struggled with this new concept. He reverted to his pre-born again prejudicial state so Paul had to withstand him telling him it was wrong. If we are one body in Christ Jesus, we should work together as one unit, one force pulling souls out of the fire.

Let's keep our mind on the things of God, and get back to the ships...

So if God Almighty sent ships to bring Africans to salvation, we perhaps need not repent for God! Here we see another side of God. He is a jealous God. He does not like to be replaced by idols. He will punish those who have other gods before Him. However, He'll not leave them there but will send rescue ships to the sinner from being eternally lost. God used France, England and the United States to bring liberation and deliverance for blacks. The United States however, has been blamed for being the alleged originator of slavery. History proves quite the contrary.

Rev. Carter notes that many prophecies were fulfilled through the sending of the slave ships. He brings his readers to another scripture in Ezekiel who prophesied further, ***"And I will scatter the Egyptians among the nations, and will disperse them through the countries"*** (30:23). History confirms that Africans were scattered hither and thither. The Lord knew that through this dispersion, liberty would be found, and eventually the gift of salvation would be offered to all Africans.

Rev. Carter ends saying that the Lord told him to tell the people that He [God] did it. He did it because He loved them. Those whom he loves, he chastises. ***"For whom the Lord loveth***

he chasteneth, and scourgeth every son whom he receiveth," (Hebrews 12:6). Carter believes that God won't back down from the reality of what he did. So an apology isn't in order according to the Reverend, but the *respect* due to all that have been created in the image of God.[9] Carter's point of view, as sensitive as it is, fits respectably into our discussion of slavery.

In the next chapter we'll continue to follow the slave dispersion. We'll see how it relates with the significance to black ladies hair and them being in slavery.

---

[1] Tom Feelings, *The Middle Passage*, (Dial Books, New York, 1995) p84 & p138.
[2] John S. Mbiti, *Introduction to African Religion, 2nd Edition,* (Heinemann International Literature & Textbooks 1975) p180.
[3] Merrill F. Unger, *Unger's Bible Dictionary* (Moody Press, Chicago, 1957) p695.
[4] John S. Mbiti, *Introduction to African Religion, 2nd Edition,* (Heinemann International Literature & Textbooks 1975) p184.
[5] Earl W. Carter Sr., "Should America Apologize for Slavery?" *Charisma Magazine*, April 1998, p82.
[6] Earl W. Carter Sr., *No Apology Necessary, Just Respect*, (Creation House, 1997).
[7] Ibid.
[8] Ibid.
[9] Ibid.

PICTURE CREDITS:
Map 2—Reader's Digest, *Atlas of the Bible*, (Reader's Digest Association, Inc., New York, 1991) p64.

Defining myself, as opposed to
being defined by others,
is one of the most difficult challenges I face.
—Carol Moseley-Braun (1947-)
Quotes from Famous Black American

Chapter 6

Your History Speaks

The commandments of God found in Deuteronomy 28, were very specific for those not to ***"go after other gods to serve them"*** (v. 14). Those who chose not to hearken unto God or observe his commandments would have a myriad of curses beset them. Idolatry and the practice of false religion were the first avoidance set in order with the building of the nation of Israel. God almighty issued a warning of all whom didn't follow his ways.

The judgement of God was not only an isolated event towards the nation of Israel but also Egypt (Africa in general) who later was scattered and dispersed by God. Many other nearby ancient nations that turned their back against the One True God oddly enough have disappeared from existence. We can only find remote artifacts from unearthed ruins today.

Without trying to be redundant, an overview of the diaspora of the slaves would be helpful. First of all, the word "diaspora" according to the dictionary refers to the period of time when the dispersion of Jews was exiled to Babylonia. This time period during the sixth century BC brought about the Talmud and added laws of Judaism. The term "Diaspora" has been used more recently in African history referring to the slave trade period.

We understand that African Diaspora is a direct consequence of the judgement of God as stated earlier. Adversities, pestilence, disunity to name a few, are results that run rampant in the countries of Africa. The passage of Isaiah, which we read previously was quite clear that ***brother*** would be ***against brother, every one against his neighbor, city against city*** (Isa. 19: 2). This explains why the tribal contention is perhaps so pervasive and continues today.

By the year 1460 AD, 700 to 800 African slaves were being transported to Portugal annually. Thus, the Diaspora fulfills prophetic scriptures found in Isaiah. In addition, they were carried not only to North America but also to South America and the Caribbean Islands. During the 400 years of African slave trade there was an estimated 12 to 13 million blacks scattered all over the earth.

Some African civilizations during the Middle Ages (Map 3)

Remarkably, Africa was quite a powerful continent. From the time of ancient Egypt, 3000BC to the fall of Timbuktu in AD 1600's she made her mark in the world. Many societies grew from small village kingdoms into complex empires through commerce, trade and warfare.[1] African chiefs and kings *(oba)* sold their prisoners of war from rival tribes to Portuguese slave traders. Benin flourished from its greatest source of money that came from the slave trade. The time frame was from the 14th to the 17th century. This east Nigerian city, later called "city of blood," got it name because it was steeped in human sacrifices. And the blood usually came from unruly slaves.

Benin city, founded about 900 AD, survived on a major trade route, which its merchants dealt in cloth, ivory, bronze, palm oil, pepper, and *the peddling of slaves*. Ironically, Benin reached its height during the reign of Oba Ewuare the Great, who ruled from 1440 to 1481.[2] This is right around the time when the slave trade of Africans began in full force. Merchants grew rich through buying and selling, so to insure the safety of their wealthy gain, they simply deposited in the newly invented Banking system.

Driven by greed Africa provides her people for the slave trade (Picture 1)

Many Africans became quite wealthy from selling their own village people to foreigners.

Historian Jeffrey Stewart tells us, "It is a myth that most Africans who became slaves in America were captured by Europeans in slave raids. Most of the Africans who became slaves were sold into slavery by other Africans."[3] History records that only a small few coastal regions were under rule of the

British, Dutch, French, and Portuguese ordinances. Europeans virtually knew nothing about the interior of Africa. The "Dark Continent," often referred to by Europeans, was not looked into until 1850 when a number of explores followed the major rivers into the center of Africa.[4] By this time America and England already began its distaste for slavery.

The East Indies had a rich supply of spices valuable for trade by the Portuguese. Later they monopolized these spices from the British and Dutch. From Africa, the Portuguese took the gold and slaves to work on the sugar plantations. After a slave revolt on the island of Sâo Tomé, the Portuguese went to set up sugar plantations across the waters in Brazil. This is how the Africans came to South America by the boatloads.

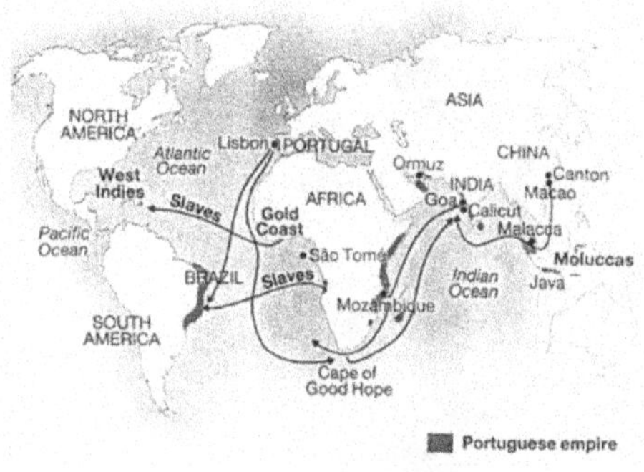

Trade Routes of the Portuguese Empire (Map 4)

Spain, desiring to rival the Portuguese, sent the Italian explorer, Christopher Columbus to find a shorter route to China but he subsequently discovered America. By 1507, Africans had arrived in the West Indies as slaves by the hand of John Hawkins. He bought slaves in Sierra Leone, Africa, and took them to Hispaniola in the West Indies where he traded them for hides and sugar. He sold these goods in England for such a profit that in 1562, Queen Elizabeth I invested money in his next voyage.[5]

Slavery was an integral part to the ever-growing plantation establishments in both Americas. In Europe, tea and coffee were the newly fashionable drinks and this gave rise to a huge new demand to sweeten the drink with sugar. Sugar grew well in the climate of the West Indies. At the end of the 17th century, about 90 percent of the West Indian people had originally come from West Africa.

By conquering the Aztecs and the Incas, Spain increased its empire. The population of the colonies grew steadily with the arrival of people from Spain. The Spanish exploited gold and silver from the New World. They forced the Native Americans to mine silver and work as slaves. It was impossible to prevent the ruling Spaniards from cruelly treating the mineworkers. Their greed drove slaves to extreme measures. As a result, thousands died because they had no resistance to European diseases such as measles and smallpox. From 1519 to 1600 the population of Mexico dropped from 25 million to just over one million.

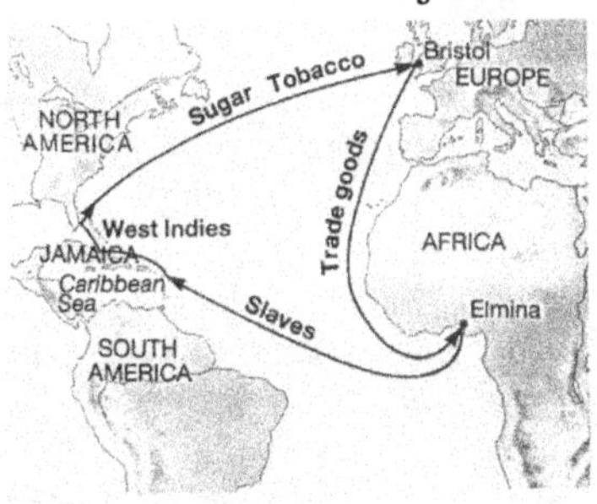

Slave Trade Triangle—(Map 5)

In the meantime, the Africans were continually torn from their normal surroundings, and put into lands foreign to their own. The Native Americans, on the other hand, were said to have made terrible slaves. They were on their own turf and knew the land. They escaped out of the hands of their oppressors into the densely wooded forests. This was not the case however for the African slave; he had never seen the vast forestland of America or the tropic land of the Indies.

By 1619, African slaves arrived to work on the first tobacco and cotton plantations in Jamestown, Virginia. Many people were ill-treated and suffered from disease and died. When the ship of human cargo arrived, they were evaluated for their strength and potential work capabilities then put up for sale on the auction block. Well-to-do plantation owners living in the southern colonies bought the majority of slaves. Approximately 10,000 plantation owners made up the ruling class in the South who owned over 50 slaves each.[6]

After being shipped here in the Americas for over four centuries the men and women of Africa had to adjust to the environment to survive. Adaptation was one of their strongest qualities. However, what were some of the results of African enslavement? Is there a relationship between slavery and black ladies hair? How did the Diaspora affect the African lady? Did a mixture of white and black genes bring about new hair types and textures? Let's explore some of the questions in our next chapter.

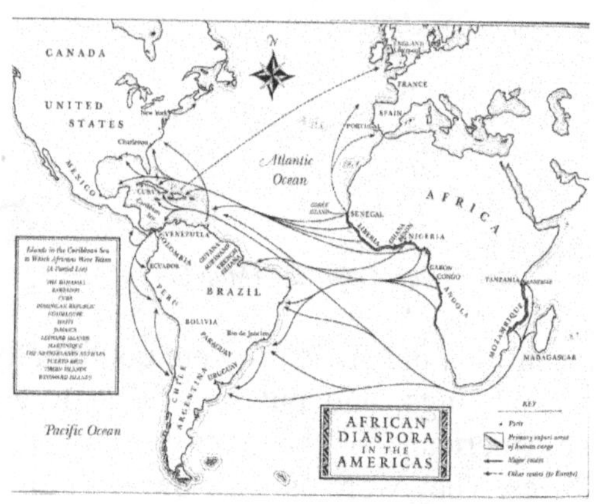

Slave Route during the Diaspora—(Map 6)

[1] "The African Past", *The New Book of Knowledge, Russell L. Adams, Chair, Department of Afro-American Studies, Howard University,* Martha Glauber Shapp, (ed.) (Danbury: Grolier Publishing Company, 2003) p79d.
[2] Tom Feelings, *The Middle Passage*, (Dial Books: New York, 1995) p280.
[3] Earl W. Carter Sr., "Should America Apologize for Slavery?" *Charisma Magazine*, April 1998, p76.
[4] Tom Feelings, *The Middle Passage*, (Dial Books: New York, 1995) p596.
[5] Ibid p366-367.
[6]"The Slave Trade", *The New Book of Knowledge, Russell L. Adams, Chair, Department of Afro-American Studies, Howard University,* Martha Glauber Shapp, (ed.) (Danbury: Grolier Publishing Company, 2003) p79e.

PICTURE CREDITS:

Map 3-- Tom Feelings, *The Middle Passage*, (Dial Books, New York, 1995) p281.
Picture 1—Ibid., p463.
Map 4—Ibid., p352.
Map 5—Ibid., p451
Map 6—Ibid., Inside cover.

There will always be men struggling to change,

and there will always be those who

are controlled by the past..

—Ernest J. Gaines (1933-)

Quotes from Famous Black Americans

Chapter 7

Slave Hair

"Man is born free," wrote Jean-Jacques Rousseau in his article, *The Social Contract*, 1764, "but everywhere he is in chains." The writings of Rousseau were pivotal for the North Americans and the French to begin to ponder the evils of slavery. He believed that slavery had no place in these nations that were formed to protect human rights. Rousseau's ideals sparked inspiration for people to fight for freedom on behalf of others who where unable to help themselves. The moral argument however couldn't win over the force generated behind the ever-growing lucrative profits of slavery.

It wasn't until 1807 that William Wilberforce led a British anti-slavery campaign. After twenty years of persuasion, he finally convinced Parliament to make new laws to abolish slavery in England. The real battle came when they had to stop the slave ships from landing in their ports. In a short time, other countries began to follow Britain's good example. God began turning the massive wheels of freedom for the slaves.

Although united in name, America was divided. The North was strong in trade, industry, and commerce while the South was a vast landscape of farmlands peppered with plantations that relied on slave labor. Laws for the new states caused sharp contention between the two American rivals. The Civil War began when forces of the South opened fire on Fort Sumter, North Carolina in 1861.

The President issued the Emancipation Proclamation on January 1, 1863, which allowed slaves to fight in the Union Army. The North victoriously won the biggest battle of the war in Gettysburg, Pennsylvania. Abraham Lincoln then gave his famous "Gettysburg Address" delivered at the dedication of a cemetery here on November 19, 1863.

Finally, four months later with many of the Southern states in ruins, and men outnumbered, exhausted and starving, General Lee surrendered to the tough and determined Ulysses S. Grant in the courthouse at Appomattox, Virginia on April 9, 1865, thus ending the Civil War. The great day of freedom came for the slaves, yet five days later; the nation lost its deliverer through an assassin's bullet. John Wikes Booth shot Abraham Lincoln to death in a Washington, D.C theater.

"The end of the Civil War, and the end of slavery marked a new beginning for American democracy," states Susan Altman in her book, *Extraordinary Black Americans*. She recalls the words of Tom Taylor, a black Civil War soldier saying, "The old flag never did wave right, there was something wrong about it. There wasn't any star in it for the black man...But since the war, it's all right. The black man has his star; it is the big one in the middle."[1]

Though on the offset one would think that the life of the slave was tenebrous and obscure but the opposite is true. The most admirable trait of the African Americans was the fact that they could adjust to their surroundings. They developed a certain aspect of slave culture that gives one a sense of their own proper dignity or value.

"In the years before the Civil War, one of the few areas in which whites allowed African Americans a relatively unhindered scope for cultural expression was the styling of hair," said authors Shane White and Graham White in their article, "Slave Hair and African American Culture in the Eighteenth and Nineteenth Centuries," printed in *The Journal of Southern*

History.[2] African American hair styling had not yet received any negative connotations.

The practice of grooming and styling of hair were the cultural rituals of the Africans. It was the texture of African hair that allowed these cultural and social practices to develop.[3] John Thornton, a historian has observed, "the tightly spiraled hair of Africans makes it possible to design and shape it in many ways impossible for the straighter hair of Europeans."[4] However, the duties of the slaves were so demanding that they often lacked the time needed for such elaborate hairstyling.

The rigors of the slave trade allowed no one to "pack a bag" or bring with them the toiletries necessary for a life-long stay in the Americas. Generally, the native was used to the African pick, or comb, whose long, smooth teeth did not snag or tear thick, tightly curled hair. "As a result," informs Willie Morrow in her book, *400 Years without a Comb,* "slaves' hair often became tangled and matted."[5] This was particularly true of the field slaves whose typical labor regime was from sun up to sun down. It made adequate care for her hair all but impossible.

The only day off was Sunday. Thankfully, slaves could find time for grooming and styling their hair with whatever implements they could find. In a slave narrative, Jacob Stroyer, former South Carolina plantation worker recalls, "before inspection by the plantation owner, attempts were made to straighten out our unruly wools with some small cards, or Jim-crows," as they were called.[6] Another former slave said, "we carded our hair caze we never had no combs, but de cards dey worked better. We used de cards to card wool wid also, and we jes wet our hair and den card hit. De cards dey had wooden handles and strong steel wire teeth." The cards referred to here were the brushes used for brushing finished cloth to get a wooly surface.[7]

In order to preserve the newly brushed tangle-free hair, the lady would "wrap" or "thread" small clusters of hair sectioned with cotton or some other material to keep it from knotting. Slave women would then wrap a head rag or bandanna around their head. They found it to be easily maintained during the workweek.

The only time bandannas would come off were on Sundays or other special occasions such as weddings or camp meetings. The small clusters of hair were released producing a nice curl. It would be brushed into a desired shape. Some slave women would simply straighten their hair by greasing it and applying a heated cloth. They found that the more straightened or relaxed the hair was the less snarled it would become.

Originated by the American Indians, the African Americans adopted this practice in the nineteenth century. James Adair, who lived as a trader among the Cherokee, Catawba and Chickasaw between 1735 and 1768 recorded, "that various tribes especially among the females would have their hair to be shining with bear's oil or grease. They reckoned it to be very valuable."[8]

Gus Fester, a former slave born in 1840, quaintly describes the images he saw of women getting ready for camp meeting. He said, "slave women took dey hair down out'n de strings fer de meeting. In dem days all de darky wimmens wore hair in strings [threads] 'cep' when dey 'tended church or a wedding. At de camp meetings de wimmens pulled off de head rags [bandannas] fresh laundered." Amos Lincoln explained the purpose of threading this way: "d' gals uster dress up come Sunday. All week dey wear dey hair all roll up wid cotton dat dey unfol' 'd cotton ball. Sunday come dey comb out dey hair fine. ...Dey want it nice an' nat'ral curly. Monday dey put d' cotton string back so it hab all week t' git curly ag'in." Oliver Blanchard concurred: "I t'ink it eel fish w'at dey strip the skin off dey back and wrap dey hair 'roun' wid it. Dat mek hair pretty and curly."[9]

Thus, head rags or bandannas became a part of the slave woman's every day attire. Some received handkerchiefs as

Christmas gifts or gratuities. Later, slave women who worked in the plantation textile manufacturing areas acquired fabrics to make for themselves headkerchiefs. Soon, a source of pride for the older women was wearing a dress with a matching bandanna.

In most cases, the head covering had strong utilitarian functions. It afforded some protection from the sun, and kept the hair clean, while helping preserve patterns of braiding and wrapping. For some African American women who lacked the implements and the leisure time to create intricate coiffures the bright colored bandanna or headkerchief became an alternate means of self-adornment and aesthetic display.

Disheveled or dirty hair, was especially for the African American woman to be a particular cause of shame, consequently the bandanna was used to hide this malady. Anthropologist Sylvia Ardyn Boone, in her study of women in West Africa, noticed preeminent cultural significance of female hair. She writes, "In West African communities admired a fine head of long, thick hair on a woman." If one had this type of hair it was intimately associated with the ideal of beauty. "Great hair is praised as *kpotongo*—literally, 'it is much, abundant, plentiful'." In addition certain cultural imperatives exist. "Women's hair must be well-groomed; merely to be presentable, clean, oiled, and plaited. For the sake of elegance and sexual appeal, hair must be shaped into beautiful and complicated styles...disheveled, neglected hair is anathema to their culture. It signified insanity." This tradition finds it morally unfitting to leave the hair unarranged and equates wild hair with wild behavior. Loose, unplaited hair is associated with loose morals.[10]

Boone's study shows the humiliation slave women may of felt in being prevented from grooming and styling their hair as they wished. During these times there was an unprecedented emergence of African American society. There was a mix of African and Euroamerican ways to make a new culture, a series of borrowings and blendings, that changing over time challenged the predominant influence of the white oppressors. Many of the slave owners would refer to the hair of the slave as to have a "large bushy head of hair." They often pointed out that their women slaves have "remarkable long hair or wool."

As the country's unrest became greater, and liberation of the slaves was growing more eminent, the suppression of the whites on the blacks became fiercer. In order to justify owning slaves, whites would devaluate blacks. One of the points of contention came from the differences in hair texture. Slaves were made to feel less. The reference to black hair being wool to some was a derogatory statement and suggests association with animals.

One former slave whose father was a plantation owner's oldest son, told how "Mistress uster ask me what that was I had on my head and I would tell her, 'hair' and she said, 'No, that ain't hair, that's wool.'…I had straight hair and my mistress would say, 'Don't say hair, say wool'."[11] The biggest weapon of racism is the pointing out of physical differences—their skin color, facial structure, and of course, thick curly hair. Prevailing racist ideology hung their hat of pride on this premise. What white supremacists needed to do was to read where the Bible refers to Jesus as to having hair "like wool" (Rev.1: 14).

Towards the end of slavery for the most part women were treated unkindly about their hair. Furthermore, it was the white females who meted out the punishment. In all my research I have come across no instance of an African American female cutting or shaving her own hair. Many considered it a grave offense and therefore it was used as a form of punishment. When jealous white female slave owners saw that the slave girls had pretty hair it was usually cut off and she had to walk around bald.

James Brittian remembered that his grandmother, an African-born slave, had hair that was "fine as silk and hung down below her waist," hair that made the "Old Miss" jealous of her and the "Old Master." The result was that the mistress, who was "mighty fractious," had Brittian's grandmother whipped and her hair cut off. "From that day on," he recalled "my grandma had to wear her hair shaved to the scalp." Judge Maddox, owner of a Texas plantation, "brought home a pretty mulatto girl" with "long black straight hair." His wife was skeptical that the slave had been purchased for doing fine needlework, and, as Jack Maddox, then a young slave later remembered, she waited until the Judge was away, "got the scissors and cropped that gal's head to the skull."[12]

Interestingly, in most of these incidents it was the similarity of the hair of individual slaves to white hair that was particularly unnerving to these white women. The hair texture showed proof that husbands, brothers, or sons had been illicitly visiting the slave quarters. It also suggested that, if hair were not shaven soon that temptation would be to great to resist.

As a result of the warped sexual dynamics of an antebellum plantation, the shaving of African American female's hair was usually indirectly pointed at the white slave owner by the jealous wife and not at the victim herself. These incidents occurred frequently enough to be part of the memoirs past from generation to generation.

The physical attributes of African Americans were disdained. The Eurocentric ideal of beauty was set in motion but more about that in an upcoming chapter. Many of the cruel taskmasters believed that blacks didn't even have a soul. However, the Bible teaches different, every person has a soul.
Now, this brings us to my favorite part of my research.

[1] Susan Altman, *Extraordinary Black Americans,* (Chicago, Childrens Press, 1989) p82.

[2] "Slave Hair and African American Culture in the Eighteenth and Nineteenth Centuries," *The Journal of Southern History,* Black Hair, by Shane White and Graham White, Senior Lecturers in the history department of the University of Sydney in Australia, Volume LXI, No. 1 February 1995, p48.

[3] Ibid, p50.

[4] John Thornton, *Africa and Africans in the making of the Atlantic World, 1400-1680*, (Cambridge, England and Oakleigh, Australia, 1992), p230.

[5] Willie Morrow, *400 Years Without a Comb* (San Diego, 1973), p19.

[6] Rawick, ed. *American Slave*, VII: *Oklahoma and Mississippi Narratives*, Jacob Stoyer, *My Life in the South* (Salem, Mass. 1898), p12.

[7] Ibid, p170.

[8] James Adair, *The History of the American Indians* (New York and London, 1968 [original publishing 1775]), p123.

[9] Rawick, ed. *American Slave*, VII: *Oklahoma and Mississippi Narratives*, Jacob Stoyer, *My Life in the South* (Salem, Mass. 1898), p85.

[10] Sylvia Ardyn Boone, *Radiance from the Waters*, 184-86.

[11] George P. Rawick ed., *The American Slave; A Composite Autobiography* (41 vols. and index; Westport, Conn., and London, 1972-1981), XVIII, p80 & p83.

[12] Rawick, ed. *American Slave*, Supplement, Series 1, *Mississippi Narratives*, Pt. 1, p217-18 and Supplement, Series 2, *Texas Narratives*, Pt. 6, p2531.

You have seen how a man was made a slave;

you shall see how a slave was made a man.

—Frederick Douglass (1818-1895)

Quotes from Famous Black Americans

Chapter 8

God's Great Liberation Plan

As stated earlier in chapter five, God had a precise plan for the African people to hear the Gospel of Jesus Christ and be saved. If we keep our eye on the Lord's plan of deliverance we see chronologically that the pieces of the puzzle fit ever so nicely. In doing this however, there may be a tendency to oversimplify the slavery problem or racism issue by ignoring complexities or complications. Those topics are so important that they need to be addressed on their own perhaps in another book at another time.

Jamestown was the first successful English settlement in the New World occurring 1607. The Pilgrims landed shortly thereafter at Plymouth Rock. The African slaves began being imported around 1617. While America was in her infancy God was helping this fledgling country come together. The thirteen original colonies were beginning to grow greatly in numbers.

The same hunger that drove those Pilgrims and Puritans across the vast waters to reach a new land to find freedom to worship God was still deep within their hearts. Many of the colonists were still struggling with obtaining their complete freedom of religion. All the while God was stirring our country and England to a spiritual renewal.

A few decades after the turn of the eighteenth century brought the **First Great Awakening**. This was the time when ministers began to preach fiery sermons. They realized that there was more to being Christian than *just* going to church. Many were good citizens, and lived good lives but they were not born again as the scriptures teach.

In 1734, Jonathan Edwards began to preach about salvation in his Congregational (Puritan) church. The Spirit of the Lord began to move the people deeply. God used this man to get the spiritual revival wheels turning. It swept through America and England for 30 years between 1730 and 1760.

John Wesley, founder of the Methodist Church began preaching in the churches in England. People again began to turn back to the Bible. England became a revived and changed country. The Methodists sent ministers to evangelize America. Reverend George Whitefield, a predominant preacher set sail across the Atlantic for Georgia in 1738. History records that sometimes the crowds drew 20,000 people at once. The churches could not hold the crowd so he decided to preach out in the open fields.

Whitefield believed that the gospel was for all people. His belief was strong enough for him to reach out to all—children, adults, Indians, African slaves, poor people, rich people, orphans, non-educated, and those with much education. He was especially tenderhearted toward the slaves. Whitefield convinced his friend, Benjamin Franklin to print an article in the newspaper for the colonists to treat the slaves with kindness.

Though the slaves were told they had no worth by some of their owners, Whitefield believed differently. Many times he preached directly to the slaves. He told them that they needed to come to Jesus just like everyone else. Here is what he said to them toward the end of one sermon:

> *I must not forget the poor Negroes. No, I must not. Jesus Christ has died for them, as well as for others. Nor do I mention you last, because I despise your souls, but because I would have what I shall say make the deeper impression upon your hearts. Oh that you would seek the*

Lord to be your righteousness! Who knows but that He may be found of you. For in Jesus Christ there is neither male nor female, bond nor free; even you may be the children of God, if you believe in Jesus. Did you never read of the eunuch belonging to Queen Candace? A Negro like yourselves. He believed. The Lord was his righteousness. He was baptized. Do you also believe, and you shall be saved. Christ Jesus is the same now as He was yesterday, and will wash you in His own blood. Go home then, turn the words of the text into a prayer, and intreat the Lord to be your righteousness. Even so, come Lord Jesus, come quickly into all our souls! Amen, Lord Jesus, Amen and Amen![1]

This amazing preacher, George Whitefield preached over 18,000 sermons in his lifetime to over ten million people. The best result of the First Great Awakening was that it drew the colonists together so that our young fledgling country would truly become one nation under God. People who were touched by the Great Awakening Era were quite hopeful of America's future. With God's help the social and political progress was possible.

In the meantime the northern frontier was being fought for dominance. France was vying for territory of Canada. England decided to go to war over it. The English won the victory at Quebec. France fought against the Indians, which lasted for nine years and was acclaimed in 1763. And young America was caught in the middle. Then only too soon the country was engaged in the Revolutionary War. At first it seems like she was dragging her feet in freeing the slaves but she was sidetracked with getting her political footing stable. Finally America won her Independence from England in 1776. And she was a free independent country.

Now, let's take a closer look at the lives of the slaves during this time. Christian missionaries were sent from the Church of England to America. In 1701, they petitioned the colonists to allow them to "bring Christ to the Africans" on the plantations. Most slaveholders resisted at first but missionaries convinced them that Christianized slaves make more reliable workers. As the fires of revival swept through the land, doors were being opened up for the African Americans. They too, were soon to be touched by the power of God.

People were so moved by the preaching and the spirit that they felt in the meetings that they didn't want to go home. They camped all night just to hear more of God's word in the morning time. This went on for weeks. Thus, the idea of the "camp meeting" was born. It is said, that even Frontiersman Daniel Boone invited the preachers to come so that he too could hear the Word of God.

In a small parish located in South Carolina, St. Helena Church opened a school and offered religious instruction to 130 Africans on their plantations. They were taught to read the Bible. The Word of God began to work in the hearts of the African Americans. In the south large amounts of slaves accompanied their masters to the rousing camp meetings and revivals hosted by Baptists and Methodist preachers. Slaves in particular, repressed in so many ways, found a welcome outlet in the movement's joyous message of salvation.[2] While perhaps they were there just to carry the luggage of the white master, they heard the preaching of God's Word. Not only heard what the preacher said, but mixed it with faith and believed. God filled many slaves with the baptism of the Holy Ghost. Now, how could this be if they didn't have a soul? It's obvious. Africans indeed, have a soul!

The **Second Great Awakening** (1830's) brought about a rise of Evangelicalism in this country. America was now a growing Protestant country. It seemed that she was in a state of constant spiritual ferment during the early years of the nineteenth century. God used Charles Finney to bring about a wave of revival. The northern part of the country, namely Rochester, New York was moved tremendously. Thousands of people were turned to Christ.

Finney preached to reach the hearts of the people rather than to their mind that housed the doctrine of reason. He simply wanted his converts to feel the power of Christ and become new men and women. He believed that it was possible for redeemed Christians to be totally free of sin—to be perfect, as their Father in Heaven is perfect.[3]

Many new churches and congregations were springing up everywhere. A new ethic of self-control and self-discipline was being instilled in the middle class. It equipped individuals to confront a New World of economic growth and social mobility without losing their cultural and moral bearings.[4]

The Shakers were a sect officially known as the Millennial Church or the United Society of Believers that came into being in 1837. Their religious services were known to become "wildly ecstatic." Their worship would begin mild but transitioned into spontaneous and violent "shaking and turning." In almost every service, members fell into trances, spoke in foreign tongues, and gave tongues and interpretation of tongues.[5] The American revival fires had touched them too! Historians record that their spiritual fervor eventually died out around 1845, but their standard of living and way of life has lasted up to these modern days.

It was a time in history when the whole country seemly was ignited with spiritual fire from heaven. Religious revivalism had swept across the land. Whites and blacks alike would gather in a clearing in the woods by the light flickering torches. Immersed themselves in cathartic outpourings of singing, shouting, and testifying about their spiritual experiences. Slaves would accent their conversation by call and response dialogues, which was an ancient African tradition. The clapping of the hands and rhythmic striking of other body parts with open palms (body percussion) was carried over from their ancestry.

The blacks too, wholeheartedly embraced the message of the gospel. Along with the whites, they too were converted. In 1758, the first known black church sprang up called "Bluestone" Church, later known as the African Baptist. History records thousands of slaves were converted to Christianity.

Testifying or telling the story of one's encounter with God was an important aspect of the African American religious experience. Through the grace of God and the power of His spirit the slaves were able to merge their own unique blend of African American Christianity. In the book, *Cut Loose Your Stammering Tongue, Black Theology in the Slave Narratives*, Will Coleman points out that it was an "organic syncretism that enabled slaves to combine their Afrocentric religious beliefs with the Eurocentric ones of their masters."[6]

The conversion experiences in the slave narratives are described as "coming through 'ligion." Coleman captures a first hand experience of a slave woman, Mary Gladdy. He states, "her memories of religious worship during the Civil War are interesting and significant. She recalled that during those days it was a difficult time. It was customary among slaves to gather together secretly in their cabins two or three times each week and hold prayer and "experience" meetings.

A large pot was always placed against the cabin door to keep the sound of their voices from escaping. Then slaves would sing, pray, and relate experiences all night long. Their great soul-hungering desire was freedom. It was not that they loved the Yankees or hated their masters, she explained. They merely longed to be free and hated the institution of slavery. Nearly always at these meetings every Negro attendant felt the spirit of the Lord "touch him just before [the break of] day."

Mariah Barnes, former slave of Seaboard, South Carolina wrote:

> *I sets here 'mongst my rags and soot and gits so happy sometimes I jes 'bound to shout. I shouted de other night in bed. In de kitchen cookin' my little piece o' flour bread, in de gyarden workin' out greens, in de bed—wherever de grace o' God swells up inside me I git so overjoyed I bound to praise my God. De slaves was all mighty proud to be free, mighty proud. Some of de marsters was good, and some was mean. Sometimes, deye' strip de slaves and whup deir backs till dey'd cut de blood out and den throw a bucket o' salt water over de raw backs. Dey made some of 'em plow all day and spin two ounces o' cotton at night. De slaves didn't git no flour bread, not even seconds; dey had to eat de grudgin's. And dey wa'n't 'lowed to meet to pray and shout neither; so dey'd have to slip off atter dark to one o' de houses and hold de prayer meetin's. Dey turned a big wash pot over close to de door, a little off'n de floor, so it'd ketch all de sound. Den de slaves'd shout and pray all dey pleased; every now and den one would slip out side to see if de pot was ketchin' all de sound. Sometimes when one would git so full o' the grace o' God and raise de shout too high, de other slaves'd throw him down on de bed and kiver up his head so he couldn't be hearn outside.*[7]

Though some slaves were taught to read the Bible many were not. Some were prohibited from reading the scriptures. Often what they received was selective parts of catechisms from either Euro-American masters and/or preachers. When they were permitted to do so, or did so secretly, they gravitated towards those scriptures that called for a radical break from old patterns, and worldly norms.

During this time freemen (slaves who bought their freedom) believed to be called to preach began to travel from plantation to plantation. Ned Walker, Henry Evans, Lemuel Haynes, and Harry Hosier were among the many whom preached the Gospel. In 1831 however, after a slave revolt led by Nat Turner, slaveholders sought to suppress preaching by blacks.[8] From then on whites periodically monitored the meetings and church services.

Many longed to be freed from the bondage of slavery. So much so that many of the newly forming black churches focussed their theology on "freedom only." Their religious services became planning meetings of revolt. And when the white slave owners found this out, some black churches were severely scrutinized or shut down completely.

When the proclamation of gospel was declared and sin was preached against [e.g. fornication, drunkenness, dancing, gambling, swearing] many of the slaves couldn't help but observe the hypocrisy and imbalance of the white slaveholders. John Pobee in his book, *Toward an African Theology: Sin and Evil in An African Theology*, states, "these range of moral offenses divert attention from those areas where ethical inspection would create tensions for the smooth operation of the system. In any authentic biblically based African theology the vertical and horizontal dimensions of religion and sin have to be held the same."[9]

In other words, Pobee was saying that the moral offenses of obvious sin (sins of the flesh) were concentrated on so that if one really looked into the Christian ideology at that time they could see that the cruelty of slavery was just as sinful and overtly wrong. Being treated as mere chattel was never justified in the Bible. This hypocrisy became more evident as African

Americans became learned in God's word and discovered its truth for themselves.

For some newly African American Christians there was a bit of confusion. They saw the inconsistency of the white Christians. Blacks read in the scriptures that instruct God's church to love one another. When they looked around they saw only hate and prejudge in the name of Christianity. It was the key factors in a slanted belief system that some of the whites soon wanted to forget. *He is a liar who professes to love God but hates his fellowman (1 John 4:20).* God's Word declares it so…and there is no doubt to that truth.

Surely all whites didn't hate all blacks and vice versa. But unredeemed whites were trying fiercely to suppress the freedom of blacks. With the tension growing on both sides, there had to be a power greater than mankind to rescue each out of the muddy waters of prejudice.

According to Dianna L. Hayes, Ph.D., S.T.D in her book, *And Still We Rise, An Introduction to Black Liberation Theology*, it states, "as slavery gave way to a freedom that too often, especially in the South, proved in its own way to merely be symbolic, the experience of Christ as Liberator was severely challenged."[10] The freedom the Black church experienced was still limited to a white dominant society.

For many slaves the gospel was a gospel of liberation. There was a deeper insight that perhaps the newly converted African American didn't see. It was a spiritual liberation going on in the inside of his heart. Before God would free the black man of his physical bondage to slavery, the Lord's desire would be to free the African first of his soul's bondage to sin (Romans 3:23).

Tom Skinner reminds us of this very point in his book, *How Black is the Gospel,* Skinner states that all unredeemed people are in a sense, in bondage. He says, "Christ did not come to save society but to redeem individuals from the curse of sin. Before coming to Christ, everyone—black and white, is in slavery to somebody or something. Some people are slaves to their money, some people are slaves to social position, some people are slaves to their family, some people are slaves to their cars or their homes, some people are slaves to their jobs."[11] Many people are slaves to drugs, alcohol, pornography, adultery, homosexuality you name it, it's out there…If we let Jesus Christ, who is King, live and reign in our life, we can be set free from the curse of sin. We then, in essence switch masters and become his slaves. And that's all right! He's a good taskmaster. *For his yoke is easy and his burden is light (Matthew 11:30).*

What a great God to include the people of Africa to taste and see that the Lord is good. He was too good of a God to leave Africa in her sinful state. But he brought her over via the ships so that she could indeed receive the Holy Ghost, and become redeemed from original sin and find true liberation in her soul and spirit. God truly had a great liberation plan for his people in Africa. He did not leave them in bondage but freed them through the power of His Spirit. I'm glad He did.

Perhaps this book would be incomplete without some black church history. Richard Allen, a black evangelist established the Bethel African Methodist Episcopal Church in Philadelphia, the city of brotherly love. He chose the Methodist faith mainly because of its strong stance against slavery.

The Baptist organization sprung up during this time also. The First African Baptist Church was established in Savannah, Georgia in 1795. By 1870 many churches grew in the number of congregates. Many camp meetings over the next two decades enjoyed interracial interdenominational gatherings. These meetings emphasized sanctification, or holiness in thought and behavior. One of the best-known evangelists, in the Holiness movement and a member of the African Methodist Episcopal Church was a lady by the name of Amanda Smith.[12]

In Holiness meetings during an ordinary worship service, fervent praying, singing, passionate preaching, dancing and other forms of physical exuberance, along with shouting and testifying were the norm. A Baptist preacher Charles Harrison, who was dismissed for his holiness beliefs, broke away and started a Holiness Church in the town of Lexington in 1897. He called the new body of believers the Church of God.

Ten years later the Church of God was change to the Church of God in Christ (COGIC). Many of their congregations received the baptism of the Holy Ghost and later became the largest black denomination. The phenomenon of Pentecost experienced by the Azusa Street Mission in 1906 sparked a new Christian movement. William Joseph Seymour, a black ordained Holiness minister and fiery preacher declared God's word and turned his world upside down.[13]

Pentecostalism didn't just stay within the black communities but was experienced by whites. African Americans invited white people into the services and insisted on interracial participation so that they too could experience this blessing from God.

Later Seymour used the word "apostolic" in the name of his church, "Apostolic Faith Gospel Mission." He considered himself and his congregation Pentecostal, distinct from Holiness congregations that did not believe that speaking in tongues was necessary for salvation. Parham, a white man, had been Seymour's teacher and mentor. He did not like the emotionalism associated with speaking in tongues and the exuberant music.

Parham and many other whites withdrew in 1908, and formed a new congregation called the Assemblies of God. It was finally fully established in Hot Springs, Arkansas in 1914.[14] Afterward, over 300 people came together to establish some set resolutions at the first general council. A few years later, another organization Pentecostal Assemblies of the World came into being to attempt to promote racial harmony.[15]

In the next chapter we will back up chronologically and focus on a time in history after the Civil war up to the turn of the twentieth and it's affects of the African American women and their hair.

---

[1] Judy Hull Moore, *The History of Our United States*, (A Beka Book, Pensacola Christian College, Florida 1998) p134.
[2] Roxie France-Nuriddin, Senior Director, *African American: Voices of Triumph*, (TimeLife Books, New York, NY,1994) p123.
[3] Robert Divine, T. H. Breen, *American: Past and Present, Vol. To 1877*, (Scott, Foresman and Company, Glenview, ILL,1984) p300.
[4] Ibid, p303.
[5] Ibid, p308-309.
[6] Eds. Dwight N. Hopkins and George C.L. Cummings,*Cut Loose Your Stammering Tongue, Black Theology in the Slave Narratives*, Will Coleman (Orbis Books, Maryknoll, New York, 1991) p68.
[7] Ibid, p88-89.
[8] *A Gallery of Antebellum Preachers*, p142.
[9] John Pobee, *Toward An African Theology: Sin and Evil in An African Theology*, (Abingdon, Tenn., 1997) p105.
[10] Dianna L. Hayes, Ph.D., S.T.D, *And Still We Rise, An Introduction to Black Liberation Theology*, Howard University Library (Paulist Press, New York, 1996) p98.
[11] Tom Skinner, *How Black is the Gospel?* (J.B. Lippincott, Philadelphia and New York, 1970) p15, p111.
[12] "The Black Church," *African Americans: Voices of Triumph*, (New York: Time Life Inc. 1993) p131.
[13] *A Gallery of Antebellum Preachers*, p153.
[14] Horace C. Boyer, *How Sweet the Sound: The Golden Age of the Gospel*, (New York: Elliott & Clark Publishing, 1995) p15.
[15] James L. Tyson, the Early Pentecostal Revival, (Hazelwood: Word Aflame Press, 1992) p195.

I can accept failure.

Everyone fails at something.

But I can't accept not trying.

—Michael Jordan (1963-)

Quotes from Famous Black Americans

Chapter 9

The Amazing C. J. Walker

After being bought and sold for 400 years, black women were merely treated as property. However, when the Civil War was ended some things changed dramatically. The blacks were suddenly set free in a hostile environment. Were would they go? Where would they live, or where would they find work? The years following the Civil War brought on much unsurety for the blacks in America. Many were born here yet didn't know whether to return to their ancient land, migrate north or just stay put. Jobs were scarce. Money was hard to come by. Disparity was certain but yet, the Lord had his hand on this newly liberated people.

During the time of slavery the black woman was told she was ugly. In order to become less attractive in most homes she was made to wear a bandana or rag on her head. Earlier, we discovered (Chapter 7) that the head covering was a very useful article of clothing. She lacked the time needed to fix her hair mainly because of the stringent tasks put on her. Consequently, her neglected hair was just covered up day after day and kept out of harms way until she got some free time to wash and fix it properly.

In a short span of forty-two years God raised up a woman to begin to restore value in the African American woman. Madam C.J. Walker was used by God to bolster confidence and self-esteem during a time when the black woman did not feel valued in American Society. Her business boomed and she became the first self-made female millionaire in United States history.[1]

She went door to door selling her own line of hair care products. She started salons to train women how to take care of their hair. She encouraged women to take pride in their appearance and to give their hair its proper attention. She invented a method using hot combs, curlers and pomades—instead of a hot flat-iron to soften and smooth black women's hair. Women were excited at the opportunity it afforded them.

Meanwhile, racism began to rear its ugly head. Bloodthirsty hate groups began springing up across America. The devil was not going to sit around twiddling his thumbs as they wandered free. 'Ol sloughfoot was looking for ways to bring the black Americans back into captivity. KKK groups were marching in the streets spewing out hatred. They used means of intimidation. Their outfits, worn by even the youngest of the groups, were to strike fear in the hearts of many. All the while, God was working through His means to bring revival to the black communities of our land.

By this time, through way of magazines, catalogs, and newspapers, the tone for the American Eurocentric standard of beauty was being established. Blonde hair, blue eyes, thin lips, thin noses, full bosom, and a tiny waist were suddenly deemed "beautiful." Madame Walker however, pushed through these obstacles. The hate and the media bias glorified the white beauty standard. Walker, on the other hand, emphasized that black ladies have their own unique qualities without trying to imitate whites.[2]

"I want the great masses of my people," Walker once said, "to take a greater pride in their appearance and to give their hair proper attention." She insisted, "to be beautiful does not refer alone to the arrangement of the hair, the perfection of the complexion or to the beauty of the form…to be beautiful, one must combine these qualities with a beautiful mind and soul; a beautiful character."[3] Though this was Walker's life message, the growing societal view was to focus on its outward beauty only. She insisted that "loveliness" be linked to "cleanliness" rather than race [or color].[4]

"Embedded in the European value system," says Birdsell in the book *Human Evolution,* "is the idea that the color white stands for purity and goodness, and any deviations from white indicate the less than pure." He continues, "Europeans have long referred to other populations as yellow, brown, red, or black," thus "climaxing in the belief that black is particularly undesirable."[5]

One wonders if after so many years of indoctrination, that many African Americans believed in the European standard of beauty also. At the time of Madam C. J. Walker, many of the blacks accepted Europeans as authorities on who is beautiful. Sultan & Naimah Latif state in their book, *Slavery: The African American Psychic Trauma*, that they believe some blacks secretly considered their own people as less attractive, while actually admiring whites' physical features. As a result, they tended to value a white person's opinion more than a black person's opinion regarding their own attractiveness.[6]

Latif and Latif explain, "when people become convinced that their natural, God-given physical features are offensive looking, they learn to feel ashamed. The low self-esteem that results from feelings of ugliness makes it difficult for them to establish healthy relationships with others. Often they spend a lifetime trying to compensate for feelings of inadequacy."[7]

Lord to be your righteousness! Who knows but that He may be found of you. For in Jesus Christ there is neither male nor female, bond nor free; even you may be the children of God, if you believe in Jesus. Did you never read of the eunuch belonging to Queen Candace? A Negro like yourselves. He believed. The Lord was his righteousness. He was baptized. Do you also believe, and you shall be saved. Christ Jesus is the same now as He was yesterday, and will wash you in His own blood. Go home then, turn the words of the text into a prayer, and intreat the Lord to be your righteousness. Even so, come Lord Jesus, come quickly into all our souls! Amen, Lord Jesus, Amen and Amen![1]

This amazing preacher, George Whitefield preached over 18,000 sermons in his lifetime to over ten million people. The best result of the First Great Awakening was that it drew the colonists together so that our young fledgling country would truly become one nation under God. People who were touched by the Great Awakening Era were quite hopeful of America's future. With God's help the social and political progress was possible.

In the meantime the northern frontier was being fought for dominance. France was vying for territory of Canada. England decided to go to war over it. The English won the victory at Quebec. France fought against the Indians, which lasted for nine years and was acclaimed in 1763. And young America was caught in the middle. Then only too soon the country was engaged in the Revolutionary War. At first it seems like she was dragging her feet in freeing the slaves but she was sidetracked with getting her political footing stable. Finally America won her Independence from England in 1776. And she was a free independent country.

While the impact of aesthetics has had a great repercussion on the black woman, it is important to note, the white woman also has had pressure to conform to this false sense of beauty. Thank the Lord there is a safety net for the women of God, whether they be black or white. (***And be not conformed to this world: but be ye transformed by the renewing of your mind,*** *Rom 12:2*). We don't have to follow the world's ideal of beauty but only have to follow the standard set in God's Word.

Bertram D. Ashe author of "Why don't he like my hair?" written in *African American Review*, states "African-Americans, with their traditional African features, have always had an uneasy coexistence with the European (white) ideal of beauty." He continues, "for black women, the most easily controlled featured is hair. It's the only way to approximate a white female standard of beauty."[10] She couldn't necessarily change the color of her skin or her facial features but she could change her hair during a time when lengthy upswept tresses known as the Gibson girl were the "ideal" for the American woman. And making the curly hair straight was one way the Black American woman could have length enough to put her hair up.

Many black women looked down on "straightening" the hair yet yearned for it to be long and healthy. Pearle Cleage in an excerpt from *Black is a Woman's Color*, sees the "pressing of hair as 'an important ritual.'" It is not a sign of our longing to be white. It is not a sign of our quest to be beautiful. We are girls. It is a sign of our desire to be women."[11] However, Walker insisted that her hair care system was not "straightening" the hair, just good grooming practices.

With this Beauty Standard War going on, it was a perfect

springboard for Madam C. J. Walker's success. She began to lose her hair during the years working as a washerwoman. Up to this time, Sarah Breedlove McWilliams as she was previously known, had a hard working life. She toiled from the cotton fields working her way up to scrubbing laundry by hand.

This amazing woman was born in 1867 in poverty-stricken rural Louisiana. The daughter of former slaves was orphaned at age 7 yet survived with her older sister by working in the fields in Delta Mississippi. She married at 14, and only to be left a widow at 20 with a 2-year-old daughter. She traveled to St. Louis to join her four brothers who established themselves as barbers.[12] Working hard as a laundry woman, she managed to save enough money to educate her daughter. She became involved in the National Association of Colored Women and NAACP.

Newly divorced from a second husband, Charles Joseph Walker who drank heavily; she was in need for some serious relief from the stress of life. Her hair unfortunately received the brunt of the stress. Sarah began to suffer from a scalp ailment. Her hair was thin and falling out.

Madam C. J. Walker

Black women in that day used to twist their hair tightly in order to straighten it. She too fixed her hair in this fashion when she began losing her hair. This combined with a mixture of poor nutrition and bad health care was all too common for the black women of her day. Many ladies suffered from "traction alopecia" which is hair loss due to extreme tension and pulling on the hair.

At the time, Walker prayed for God's help. When she was 38 years old, a formula came to her in a dream and later was known as Wonder Hair Grower. She told her friends that, with divine help, she learned how to make the mixture she needed to grow out her hair. "God answered my prayer" she said, "One night I had a dream, and in that dream a big black man appeared to me and told me what to mix up for my hair. Some [ingredients] of the remedy was grown in Africa, but I sent for it, mixed it, put it on my scalp. And in a few weeks my hair was coming in faster than it had ever fallen out. I tried it on my friends; it helped them. I made up my mind I would begin to sell it."[13]

In 1905, she then aggressively began marketing the hair-growing mixture and two other products designed specifically for black women: glossine meant to add luster, and a substance called "Vegetable Shampoo" to strengthen the hair. [14] "If hair is what you want," declared the *Madam C. J. Walker Year Book*, "then the Walker hair preparations are what you need. If money is what you want then become a Walker agent. Write today and be convinced."[15] She offered to others also a chance to sell products as well as use them. From that point on her business grew rapidly.

She started a manufacturing company in 1910 providing job opportunities for black women while training them in her system for healthy hair care. She encouraged her agents to open their own businesses, contribute part of their earning to charities, and to take great pride in their personal appearance and to give their hair proper attention.[16]

In a short time of nine years she became very wealthy and her business was booming but her health was not. Her doctors warned her to slow down. But she would not. Walker suffered from high blood pressure and later died of kidney failure at the age of 52 on May 25, 1919. She was a great contributor to many charities and was missed greatly.

The business later fell into the hands of her attorney, her agents and her sales representatives. With hopes of her daughter and adopted granddaughter carrying on the business perhaps the Walker legacy could live on. However, this was not the case. History records that her daughter, A'Lelia became something of a Harlem girl, famous for her flamboyant style and lavish, celebrity-studded gatherings. She traveled much and spent her wealth. But that was short lived.

A'Lelia died too, middle aged suffering from a fatal stroke at the age of 46 in 1931. The Walker estate and proceeds was eventually donated to the NAACP. To date, the block-sized manufacturing building was turned into a theatre center with office buildings and known as a National Historic Landmark in Indianapolis, Indiana.

[1] African American Voices of Triumph, (eds.) (Alexandria, VA: Time-LifeBooks, 1994) p81.
[2] Madame C. J. Walker (Sarah Breedlove), *The 100 Most Influential Women of All Time,* Deborah G. Felder, (Secaucus NJ: Carol Publishing Group 1996) p306. BROWNELL LIBRARY—HOWARD UNIVERSITY
[3] *All the Rage*, p122.
[4] "Madame C. J. Walker," *Extraordinary Black Americans,* Susan Altman (ed.), (Chicago: Childrens Press, 1988) p109.
[5] Latif, Sultan A. & Naimah, "Black Beauty Standards" *Slavery: The African American Psychic Trauma, (Communications Group, Inc, 1999)* p240.
[6] Ibid, p241.
[7] Ibid, p239.
[8] Ibid.
[9] "The Role of Skin Color and Features in the Black Community: Implications for Black Women and Therapy" *Clinical Psychology Review* 9, (1989) p323-33.
[10] "Why Don't He like My Hair?" *African American Review*, Bertram D. Ashe, Volume 29, Number 4, 1995.
[11] "Black is a Woman's Color," Hairpeace, Pearle Cleage, *African American Review 27* (1993) p37-41.
[12] Madam CJ Walker-The Life of Beauty Mogel Madame Walker, http://inventors.about.com/library/inventors/blwalker.htm
[13] A'Lelia Perry Bundles, *Madam C. J. Walker Entrepreneur*, (New York: Chelsea House Publishers, 1991) p35.
[14] *All the Rage*, p121.
[15] Madam C. J. Walker Year Book and Almanac, (Indianapolis: Mme. C. J. Walker Mfg. Co, 1930) p19.
[16] Ibid, p66-67.

Racism is not an excuse to not do the best you can.

—Arthur Ashe (1943-1993)

Quotes from Famous Black Americans

Chapter 10

Tyranny of the Blonde Bombshell

By the time of Madame Walker's death in May 1919, the "Great Youth Rebellion of the 20's" was getting into full swing. Women started the hair-bobbing trend just two years prior to make a fashion statement. One would be surprised at the sharp contention that these American women stirred up when they began to wear the "boy-bob" hairstyle. This fostered fierce debate across America. The chronological disasters that followed only show you of God's disapproval of these actions. Sin was creeping into America at an alarming rate. This era opened up a floodgate of lawlessness. Here is a thumbnail sketch of what happened.

The First World War was over. United States citizens enjoyed their liberty and victory won but carried it to extremes. And with this footloose fancy-free thinking society the roaring 20's brought on much rebellion. In a short span of ten years it plummeted into the Great Depression of the 30's. And little by little, America got her mind off God. She was sidetracked from going to church to hear the Bible preached. Instead she went off on Sunday drives in the newly invented automobiles. Youth used these vehicles as a way to sneak away from watchful authority. Yet all the while, God's eyes were beholding this pitiful sight.

As our country drifted from doing what was right in the sight of God, preachers were warning their parishioners not to follow this lascivious generation. Let's remember that just fifty years prior the nation had enjoyed a notable revival throughout the land during the Second Great Awakening. But at this time America's spiritual renewal was being pulled asunder by untamed lusts. She was losing her grip on righteousness.

It was usual for America to look to England for her mores and standards of living. The queen of England ruled with a strict moral code that had a great influence on 19th-century British society. When Queen Victoria died in 1901 her son, Edward VII ascended the throne. He was known to many as a playboy. He seemly let everything go. Thankfully, he ironically ruled England for a short nine-year time span. However during his reign, he challenged the 64-year prim and proper era set in motion by his mother. Perhaps this is why revival flourished in her reign. After her death society took a nosedive and changed so quickly. Sin corrupts good manners just as ink spilt does a garment.

So during the turn of the 20th century our country was literally spilt in half, righteousness and worldliness. This behavior, women cutting their hair, became the throttle stick that caused our great nation to take a nosedive. Carnality became the norm. No doubt people wondered what's wrong with doing this thing or that. Deceptive questioning was on the uprise because society stopped reading the Word of God for guidance. They became willfully ignorant of what God required and leaned heavily on man's reasoning. Darwinism was gaining momentum. The Bible was nothing more than a decoration on the coffee table. The love of pleasure overshadowed their love for God. Perhaps they thought if everyone else was doing it didn't that make it right?

For an in depth discussion on the history of women cutting their hair and the ramifications it led to read my first book, "***My Hair, My Glory: Is there really any significance***?" For the sake of time and repetition this book will not cover that subject. But I need to add that Madam C. J. Walker also got caught up in this hair-cutting trend and did likewise.

The Eurocentric standard of beauty was steadily becoming regarded as the norm. Advertisements and magazines pushed this dogma down the throats of the American women. And though in its infancy stage, the media had a great deal of influence on people. America was slowly becoming entrenched in its trap.

The silent movie theatres were the thrill at the time. They eventually developed into the silver screen motion pictures. Actors were now heard in the picture shows. People would flock to see their performances. And so deeply was their influence over society that many wanted to be just like the movie stars. This is what started the blonde bombshell epoch.

Hollywood soon discovered how good a blonde hair actress looked in their black and white films. Mae West was one of the first bombshells to be dropped. These so-called blonde beauties popped up in numbers on the movie screens. Soon to follow was the sardonic Jean Harlow who died at a young age of 26. Some say that her death was caused by the overuse of hair dye.

Legend has it that Jean Harlow spent her days hairless and hidden beneath a white wig because too-frequent blonding caused her hair to break off in clumps.[1] The pursuit of beauty often led women to engage in health-threatening behaviors. The darker the hair the more processing it would take to achieve blondeness. It would require a double processing stripping the hair of all it's pigment (color) then adjust and add the desired shade of pale.[2]

Since light hair was the rage a host of blonde superstars were soon to follow. The culture depicted attractiveness in "blondeness." The American society's mentality was being shaped by its emphasis on physical appearance. People began equating self-worth and the worth of others with being able to attain this attractiveness.[3]

The blonding process was very dangerous at this time. It caused headaches and scalp burns from the chemicals. It was not unusual for the hair to break off during the process. The bleach formula used was a mixture of peroxide and ammonia, then ivory soap flakes were later added to make a paste. One writer stated that the peroxide stripped away the pigment as fast as a knife goes through butter.

Artists learned this process from a French chemist named Eugene Schueller who manufactured his product as early as 1907. The main ingredient he used was called paraphenylenediamine. *That stuff has some of the same corrosive chemicals they use in jet and rocket fuels.* Schueller ended up calling his company L'Oreal. Interestingly, it is still the leader in hair dye solutions. His predecessor, I read in the newspaper a few years back, inherited his fortune and is listed as one of the top ten billionaires in the world today.

With Hollywood's continued demand for hair dyes, an American chemist, in 1931 introduced his first oil shampoo tint. Lawrence Gelb established a home hair dye and named his company Clairol. In the Mid 30's another man, John Breck invented the retail shampoo for the public to use. He introduced his product using advertisements that featured the "Breck Girl." And you guessed it; all his models at that time were blondes. This product is still on the market today.[4]

So what was the big thrill in being blond? According to my research being blond meant being youthful looking. In the *African American Review* Winter 1995, Bertram D. Ashe writes, "that part of the white cultural ideal of femininity is the large amount of value placed upon the 'youthful beauty concept.'" He stated that "if a white female is to retain her culturally prescribed femininity, she must be relegated to a 'non-adult or child-like appearance.'"[5]

According to Stephen Chapman, in his article "Dark Women Rule—What's with America's fixation on blondes?" that ran in the *American Spectator* July 1996, states that it has been theorized that blondes "appeal to something deeply rooted in the male psyche by suggesting youth and innocence."[6] He noted that

98 percent of the female actresses featured in films are some shade of blonde.[7] If we were to name famous blondes the list would go on forever. Are they natural blondes? Funny, we never ask if a person is a natural brunette.

Designer William Geist affirmed that blond hair triggers madness in men. In his article on the allurement of blondes written in the *Vogue Magazine* February 1990, he says a lot of men he knows spend time fighting their natural biological bent toward blondes.[8]

Author Joanna Pitman writes in her book, "On Blondes" that blond fixation is not a recent phenomenon but dates back to the ancient days of Greece when prostitutes mimicked the golden haired Aphrodite, goddess of love. The blonde madness spectrum swings from one side of being an erotic sex symbol to the other side of being the saintly virgin.[9] When it's time to show the bad person however, the evil witch or villainess is always shown with dark hair. Blondes areoverly represented in the "good characters" of angels, saints, goddesses, and fairy godmothers.[10] Thus this stereotype has been present throughout the centuries.

The trend never really died out but was reborn and glamorized during the infancy of the Hollywood industry. Janet Siroto reports in her article "Lightening Strikes" *Vogue Beauty Magazine* January 1994, that "certainly this hair hue [blonde] has long been a foolproof attention getter."[11] Men stress attractiveness in women more than women do in men. It is understandable that women are under more pressure to conform to these beauty standards. And for the love of money, fame, and the attention they get, women are willing to offer it with dyeing their hair blonde.

Scientists to study the beauty trends did an archival research on the use of blonde models in our country. The results were eye opening. Because magazines play a vital role and send powerful messages in communicating these beauty standards to society, they served as a valuable source of data. And though there are estimated over 10,000 different magazines these researchers only used four different ones. I wonder what the other 9,996 magazines pictured?

The researchers somehow studied these trends for a four-decade period, 1950-1980. Their study may easily conclude that these images deliver a message to society that blonde is a prominent ideal of feminine beauty. Perhaps some of the contribution has been with Hollywood's early preoccupation with blondeness.[12]

Garner, Garfinkel, Schwartz, and Thompson collected data from three popular women's magazines and *Playboy* magazine and noted the upward trend of the appearances of blondes. Research stated that up to 41 percent of the centerfolds were blondes. It varied over the years but was higher than the norm and the rate of blonde models in the *Ladies' Home Journal* and *Vogue* magazines. Could the excessive use of blondes in men's magazines be why there is a "biological bend" that is "deeply rooted in the male psyche"? The worldly men have had strong messages sent to them associating female blondeness to sexuality and beauty.

Though their hypothesis was complex it showed that blondeness is a very popular tool used for selling. The results indicated that blondes surpassed brunettes and redheads in appearance for *Playboy* magazine. However, brunettes appeared more in the women's magazines, and interestingly, redheads fell to less than ten percent in all. One wonders what about all those black hair models? Were they non-existent in the magazines?

Even though there may not be as much push for blondeness today you can still feel an undercurrent pull towards being in vogue, in style or looking like the most popular model. Vickie Woods in her article "Why is hair such hell?" printed in *Vogue Magazine* October 1997, quoted many fashion stylists. One said, "unless you grasp the significance of hair, you cannot know the power instilled in it." Woods confirms "there isn't a woman in America who doesn't understand the significance of hair."[13] And because women know this truth intrinsically, there is much pressure to live up to the standard.

Many women are told that t hey need to change their hairstyle to stay up with fashion. One stylist, Garren says, "if you're in a position where you have to look groomed, you need to go to the hairdresser two or three times a week." One says, "if you're over 40 the commonest mistake is to keep your hair too long and to keep it all one color." And another says "why keep your hair gray: it drains your face."[14]

There is a constant bombardment from the worldly advertisements to change what God has given you. And without the power of the Holy Ghost to help resist this onslaught of fashion lies, many Apostolic Pentecostal women have done just what fashion gurus have chanted.

Sirto says, "platinum [blonde] hair may look right only if it doesn't stray too far from the realm of cutting-edge fashion."[15] Let me ask who are the fashion police to decide where the edge is? Someone said in an article that fashion models and movie stars have changed their hairstyle, color and length so many times it is beginning to look like a personality disorder. Being blonde isn't all what it's cracked up to be anyway. There is a lot of stigma attached to it.

Up until World War II, a woman who dyed her hair was considered "fast." Hollywood depicted the blonde as being dumb, naughty, and immoral. Clairol wanted more women to purchase their home hair dyes so they came up with famous catchy advertising slogans:

> DOES SHE OR DOESN'T SHE?
> ONLY HER HAIRDRESSER KNOWS FOR SURE. BLONDES HAVE MORE FUN!
> MEN PREFER BLONDES![16]

So suddenly the advertising trend caught on, women dyed their hair many times a year. All the while, companies were making millions of dollars. Statistics show that the number of American women who dye their hair is one in three.[17] Blonde, brunette, red or black any color seems to do nowadays.

The flip side of the blonde hair tyranny phenomenon is she was stereotyped with stupidity. Oh great, you may be beautiful and young looking but your stupid. That's a high price one must pay for beauty. Blonde jokes pegged people into holes and are very much alive today. It may be true that one in 20 are natural blondes but it's a little unbelievable that they *all* are supposedly dumb. Stereotyping is dangerous.

Novelist Kathryn Harrison wrote an article "Blond on Blond" published in *Vogue Magazine* September 1994. She was a natural born blond and smart. She said that she finds that in our culture the two traits didn't go together. All through high school she suffered the brunt of blonde jokes. She was called Cousin Itt, after that member of the Addams family because her blonde hair hung around past her waist like a curtain.

One afternoon, when she was a young adult, she was standing around at an art show reception, an attorney acquaintance walked up to her and started rapidly firing the blonde jokes. During other conversations at other occasions she noted that within minutes people would say to her, "for a blond, you're pretty smart," or they'd say, "you're so much smarter than I expected."

Comments like these, Harrison says "almost reflects an unconscious reflex of bias, they are palpably hostile." Being blond obviously caused people (mostly men) to give her a tongue-lashing. Those who voiced their comments felt like they needed to punish her for demonstrating both intelligence and blondeness. The reactions she endured made her think that she'd broken some unwritten rule. She ended her article by saying that she was glad she was now married to a man that likes a woman who is both smart and appealing.[18]

The fury over blondeness has overshadowed the African American woman. Many of the TV commercials advertising hair products never showed the black lady's hair especially in the 40's, 50's, and 60's maybe even during the height of the 70's hippie movement. Many black ladies can remember their mothers or aunts referring to hair as "good" or "bad" hair. Most young Afro-American girls grew up with a mind set that good hair was lengthy and had manageability if you were female and for males it had waves that fell just right.

In an article I found in the *Chronicle of Higher Education*, the author stated that she thought something was wrong with "us" referring to black people. The culture had conditioned many to believe, says the author, that their hair was "bad" hair. And sometimes this thinking was carried over into adulthood. For years many a man or woman painfully tried to adapt his or her hair to the Eurocentric standard of beauty. And this carried on for decades. Today however, many African Americans are slowly rejecting the notion that their physical features are ugly or bad.[19]

Ingrid Banks, author of *"Hair Matters: Beauty, Power and Black Women's Consciousness*," discusses the sensitivity of this issue. Many ladies of color are celebrating their distinctiveness by learning how to care for their hair.[20] They've learned to overcome any oversight that our culture may have inflicted. "*Nappy Hair,*" a favorite children's book, written by Carolivia Herron speaks to children of color. African American children learn from Brenda, the character of the book, about her tightly coiled hair. She talks about liking her hair. This book endeavors to dispel any kind of negative or derogatory feeling towards ethnic hair.

Without trying to oversimplify a very sensitive issue, the black lady, especially Apostolic Pentecostal, still wrestle with what is expected by God of them in regards to their hair. Very simply put, she should not do any thing that harms or abuses her glory (hair). She should be smart and ardently study books on hair that are up to date. Apostolic Pentecostal women need to reject the old notions that black hair won't grow. There are <u>many</u> black hair care books that promote proper hair care guidelines (see appendix for resource titles). More of hair care tips in the next chapter.

[1] "Lightening Strikes" *Vogue Beauty Magazine,* Janet Siroto, January 1994, Volume 184, p73-74.
[2] Ibid.
[3] "American Image of Beauty" *Sex Roles: A Journal of Research,* Melissa Rich and Thomas Cash, July 1993, Volume 29, p113.
[4] "Hair History" Kathy Rothkop Hair Design, www.hairrific.com
[5] "Why Don't He like My Hair?" *African American Review*, Bertram D. Ashe, Volume 29, Number 4, 1995, p585.
[6] "Dark Women Rule—What's with America's fixation on blondes?" *American Spectator*, Stephen Chapman, July 1996, p51.
[7] Ibid.
[8] "Blondes" *Vogue*, Phyllis Posnick, editor, February, Volume 180, 1990, p312.
[9] Joanna Pitman, *On Blondes*, (Bloomsbury New York and London 2003).
[10] "American Image of Beauty" *Sex Roles: A Journal of Research,* Melissa Rich and Thomas Cash, July 1993, Volume 29, p114.
[11] "Lightening Strikes" *Vogue Beauty Magazine,* Janet Siroto, January 1994, Volume 184, p73-74.
[12] "American Image of Beauty" *Sex Roles: A Journal of Research,* Melissa Rich and Thomas Cash, July 1993, Volume 29, p120.
[13] "Why is hair such hell?"*Vogue Magazine,* Vickie Woods, October 1997, Volume 187, p396.
[14] Ibid.
[15] "Lightening Strikes" *Vogue Beauty Magazine,* Janet Siroto, January 1994, Volume 184, p76.
[16] "Hair History" Kathy Rothkop Hair Design, www.hairrific.com
[17] Joanna Pitman, *On Blondes*, (Bloomsbury New York and London 2003).
[18] "Blond on Blond" *Vogue Magazine*, Kathryn Harrison, September 1994, p428.
[19] "Black Hair", The Chronicle of Higher Education, October 1996, p76.
[20] Ingrid Banks, *"Hair Matters: Beauty, Power and Black Women's Consciousness*, (New York University Press 2000) p1.

The battles that count aren't the ones for gold medals. The struggles within yourself—the invisible, inevitable battles inside all of us—that's where it's at.

—Jesse Owens (1913-1980)
Quotes from Famous Black Americans

Chapter 11

Beauty that Touches the Heart

Many an African American Apostolic woman has deep-rooted feelings about her hair and physical features. Perhaps even after coming to God in the fullness of salvation there has been yet another battle to conquer—psychological defeat. The woman who was conditioned to think that her hair, her countenance was less desirable and untouched by beauty to the average person has had to ask the Lord to make her thoughts to become new (Romans 12: 2).

Let me give you a positive affirmation that God almighty likes what he created. He had no problem with the way he made you. I've stated in my second book, *Daring Dos* that it's not so much what the outer world sees as is one's own mental image. It is what's going on in the *inside* that counts. In other words, it's not so much what's *on* your head as much as what's going on *in* your head that matters.

And let me remind you once again, it was sin that distorted the meaning of beauty anyway. We want to be women who worship in the beauty of His holiness (Ps 96: 9). We need to become new creatures in Christ (2 Cor. 5: 17) and not follow after the world and its ideologies. Besides, remember King Solomon's mother's admonition, ***"Charm is deceitful and beauty is vain, but a woman who fears the Lord, she shall be praised"*** (Prov 31:30).

One would never know the battle that is going on inside the head unless it's brought to our attention. With discretion it can be brought to light and discussed. "Most nonBlack Americans are unable to make an educated guess," says authors Ayana Byrd & Lori Tharps in their book, *Untangling the Roots of Black Hair in America,* "about the form or function of basic Black hair tools, style techniques, or maintenance rituals." The consequence of this has become a proverbial "secret-society status of Black hair care in popular culture."[1]

The authors continue, "compounding this problem is the average person's lack of knowledge regarding Black America's tangled hair history. There is no denying that Black hair can feel like a burden rather than a blessing. As a result, many women harbor repressed frustrations with the time, energy, and effort Black hair requires to get it into a style society deems acceptable."[2]

Gail Jacobs, a Jewish woman who has lived with two different Black women over a period of eight years agrees, she says, "Unless you live with someone who is Black, as a White person you will probably remain quite ignorant of the ways in which Black hair is different." Because of this ignorance, many Whites inquisitively ask about Black hair. The sad discovery is that innocent questions always seem loaded, and curiosity can be misconstrued as mockery. **Her Ebony Glory** hopefully erases all the misconceptions that are built up through the years.

One of the points of my endeavors is to help the Apostolic African American sister to get her hair looking it's best. Hey, you're not alone in the battle. I've seen some motley-looking White Pentecostal sisters running around. Yikes! For that reason, I wrote the book, *Daring Dos* (it has over 49 different hair dos).

At some conferences I've been to, the women's hair looked so bad that I knew they were in some serious need of help. It's the truth. Some of them perhaps hadn't seen a comb and a mirror in a month. You laugh 'cause you know I ain't lyin.' You've seen them out there too.

The Scripture says Colossians 1: 27, ***"Christ in you, the hope of glory."*** I was thinking on that scripture one day. Then the thought hit me. Perhaps God Almighty was hoping, (yea even begging) for his glory to shine through his women. But first, you need to get your glory (hair) looking its best and not looking like it blew up in a steel wool factory. Are you getting the point? God wants his glory to shine. Oh, help us Jesus!

This chapter will only scratch the surface of resource books out there for African American hair care. *See the back appendix for a complete list of titles to help your hair get growing and looking its best.* First we must get an understanding of the unique structure of African hair. My favorite drawing came from the book, "*Professional Cosmetologist.*" Author John Dalton had this sketch of the four different hair types

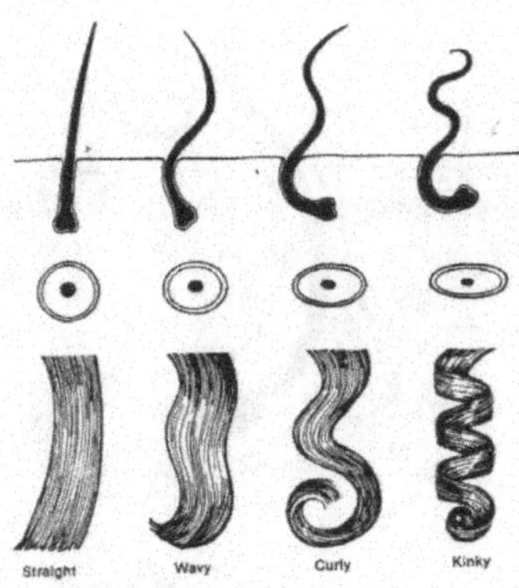

Follicles of Four Different Hair Types—Diagram 1

This picture shows the hair root from which the hair grows. The hair grows from a FOLLICLE, which is the pore or hole from which the hair emerges. After the keratinization process (forming of cells) the hardened structure is pushed through the hole to form the shape of the hair. Think of it as decorative frosting on a cake.

The cake decorator uses different tips to create a variety of shapes say on a wedding cake for example. The frosting then gets squeezed through the *tip* making a certain type of shape. This is the same idea of the hair follicle. It is the angle of the follicle that effects the configuration of the hair. Whatever the shape of follicle on your scalp determines the form or curliness of your hair.

If you were born with stick straight hair, your follicle is round. If your hair is slightly wavy your follicle looks less circle-like and has more of an oval shape. If you have curly hair your follicle is very oval looking. And if your hair is kinky with tight "s" or "z" curves your follicles have openings that look like rectangles or slots making the hair shafts flat on the sides. This is why perms and straighteners don't work...*But more about that later.*

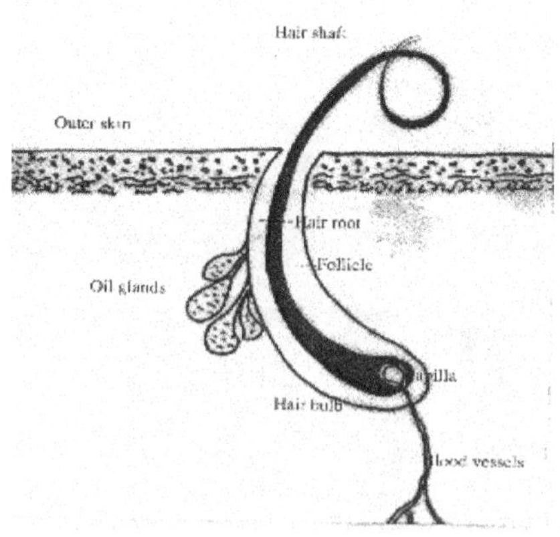

Side View of hair shaft—Diagram 2

Because of the African American's history and ethnic mix, African hair has many degrees of curliness, ranging from wavy to very tight springy coils. So in the Afro-American's case, hair on the scalp itself may be very curly with tight coils on top but toward the nape of the neck and crown of the head, the hair's curls are looser. According to Lonnice Bonner in her book, *Good Hair,* she writes, "many women with tight African hair actually have two or three degrees of curl on different parts of their scalp."[3]

In order to care for your hair Bonner states to get the best results treat Black hair like curly hair instead of always going to the extreme opposite. When a strand of unprocessed hair is pulled out, it looks like a coiled spring on a slinky toy, curled to the nth degree![4] Bonner's book is the best at answering the following questions: *Why is African hair so dry, why doesn't it shine, and why does it breaks so easily especially when chemically processed, and why does it tangle so much*...you'll find the answers in her light-hearted book (pg 19 & 20). She has done a great job and I'd hate to just plagiarize her ideas as my own. Since my research Bonner has written several books, see appendix for titles.

A word of caution here to our AAA sisters, Bonner suggests that a woman starts over from scratch and shave her head. She believes then you can start with virgin hair but I say—*DON'T DO THAT!!! God forbid.*

Many of the professionals who work with African hair say the same thing about this kind of texture: you must work with what you've got to get it to look its best. A chemical-free regimen is a superb way to keep hair healthy. The best book I found on this subject was by Pamela Ferrell. In her book, *Where Beauty Touches Me*, she states, "Lack of knowledge is the greatest cause of hair problems. Hair in these modern times is worse than in the past because of the availability of products and harmful applications by untrained and unthinking people. Having a good knowledge of your hair and how it relates to the overall health is important."[5]

Ferrell has made it her life purpose to re-educate black ladies on how to take better care of their hair. She states that many that visit her salon in Washington, DC come in when their hair is in its worst possible condition. Many of her clients need, as she puts it, "hair rehabilitation." Ferrell says her role has changed from a simple stylist to a **hair care specialist**. Twenty percent of her new clients are bald from years of hair abuse. Ninety percent of her clients who have had relaxers or perms have some form of hair damage.[6]

So what's her solution? To go natural, of course! Not in a 1960's sense when the hair was flying everywhere but to keep hair in its virgin chemical-free state. Her passion for hair cures and great care for African American women is so evident in this book. Again, I'd hate to plagiarize her ideas as my own so I'm referring you to her book. **She too, refers to cutting the woman's hair. DON'T! Just let your hair grow out naturally. Start were you're at. I had to do the same.**

Hey, let me be frank here. When I got saved my hair looked like the Indianapolis 500-speed racetrack. I let a girl from my high school cut my hair a week before I graduated. That was a BIG mistake. She messed it up royally. My hair never grew. Three years later, I got the Holy Ghost. The Sunday before the week I got saved I had an appointment for the hairdresser to get my three-inch-below-the-ear-length hair fixed. I never did go to the salon and for years I had very uneven hair. But it never bothered me. It was a testimony and I treated it as such. God eventually grew my hair out and fixed the slanted ends. God is so good.

After reading Ms. Ferrell's book, you'll come away with a renewed feeling and appreciation as to how God made you. You will be thankful for naturally kinky hair instead of thinking it's a birth defeat. Since my research Ferrell has written several books, see appendix for titles.

Andre Walker wrote the next great book I found. I love this book! He is the hairdresser of Orpah Winfrey, the billionaire talk show guru. In his book, *Andre Talks Hair,* Orpah states in the forward that hair played a prominent role in her life. As a girl she was told, "Child, your hair is your crowning glory." She recalled being told that she risked the wrath of ancestors—or worse, the living—if she dared cut it. Orpah declares she didn't cut hers for years, except to trim ends *(that's the same thing, anyway).* Hair in her world was to be revered, admired. She reiterates what has been said earlier, "it's how you feel about your hair that matters more than anything."[7] That sounds as though even Oprah had to come to grips with dealing with black hair.

Andre talks about hair in such a delightful way. He lets us in on his secrets he used on Ms. Winfrey. Here is what he said. Andre washes Oprah's hair every other day. Don't panic! I know what you're thinking: "I can't do that." Oh really, why not? Ever see Oprah Winfrey's hair bounce and blow free. It's so nice and soft looking. She has very coarse, thick hair with the zigzag pattern. He uses a protein moisturizing shampoo and conditioner that contains botanical ingredients.

That sounds like a lot but hey, I don't believe she is in that chair for more than thirty-forty minutes per day. He teaches how you could do that. Listen sisters, my hair is over four feet long and it takes me about the same amount of time on a church day. The trick is to come up with a routine that works for you.

So how does Oprah keep her hair so healthy? It's simple says Andre, "**conditioners, conditioners, conditioners**." Condition your hair to the max but (here's the tricky part) don't over condition it. You must feed your hair and keep well informed as to how to keep it healthy and soft. In a nutshell, here is what Andre recommended. First he categorizes hair into four types, stick straight, wavy, curly, and kinky hair. African hair falls into **Type Four**.

Type Four hair is ok to shampoo regularly. By doing this, it will wash away dirt and oils and actually return moisture back into the hair. Andre insists Type 4 hair must be shampooed at least once a week, twice is better, and if you have an active life, shampoo it more often. Some women don't wash it in two weeks. (*Hey, I knew a guy who didn't shower in two months. Yikes!...He wasn't in the church).*

Here are Andre's secrets: Shampooing adds much needed moisture to Type 4 hair. Wetting the hair is the ultimate moisturizer. When hair is the driest it's because it's in disparate need of a shampoo. But it MUST be a good protein based shampoo with natural ingredients such as shea butter, glycerin, sulfur, and carotene. Some biotanical ingredients are chamomile, comfrey and rosemary. READ THE LABEL. Don't buy the cheap stuff…you know, four bottles for 99 cents. If your hair is relaxed, look for products formulated for dry or chemically treated hair.

Many think that Type 4 hair lacks OIL, but this is not true declares Andre. The hair looks and feels dry because the hair's kinks and coils prevent nutrients from the scalp to distribute them evenly thoughout the hair. The oil clogs the hair follicles, making it even harder for the hair to get those natural lubrication oils and nutrients, thus making the hair even drier. The old fashion way was just to apply a hot-oil treatment. Hair unwittingly ends up oiling the scalp and clogs up the follicles blocking and stopping nutrients from flowing down each strand of hair. The result is an oily mess. The solution to this dilemma is not oil but **more moisture**.

After shampooing, you must condition hair. This can strengthen damaged hair and keep it healthy and prevent the hair *from* getting damaged. The conditioner should have lanolin and protein to moisten it. Many people think that hot oil treatments moisturize the hair but they don't. Oil and water don't mix. You can deep-condition your hair also twice a month so that hair is even more strengthened and less likely to snap and break off under pressure.

Andre has some techniques for blow-drying hair. His recommendation: hair must be clean or else you'll just bake the dirt into your hair and damage it. Type 4 hair can even be blow-dried straight—though a little tricky.[8] If straightened hair is your goal, the book mentions wet setting. Andre claims that it's one of the easiest and most lasting ways to get hair straightened. Hey, why not give it a try?

This book has a number of topics on hair care, damage control, dealing with what you were born with, and finally he answers the most common hairstyling questions. It is an excellent book, and again, for the sake of not wanting to plagiarize, I just refer you to it. I found the book for one dollar on Amazon.com. However, I must caution once again, **Andre too, refers to cutting the woman's damaged hair completely off and starting over again. I do NOT recommend this at all.**

I found a great alternative to shaving the hair. In a booklet, Looking Good Naturally put out by the Editors of *Heart & Soul Magazine.* They quote David Cannell, Ph.D., corporate vice president for technology at Redken, "you can correct hair damage and weakness [in some cases by up to 60 percent] by fortifying hair with what it needs most—scientifically formulated hair-conditioning products that are rich in protein." He says, "research reveals that hair, which is primarily composed of protein, can absorb topically applied proteins."

The Editors go on to say, "high-protein hair-care products provide a beautiful alternative to shaving our heads and starting from scratch." Many manufactures offer an Emergency Hair Repair Kit (available in salons nationwide) that features a shampoo, conditioner, and damaged-hair treatment rich in taurine, a natural amino acid that easily penetrates hair—especially damaged areas."[9] The hair recovery kit I recommend is the **Nioxin** program. They guarantee their products. I called and asked specifically, if African hair could benefit from its use. They replied "absolutely." They guarantee it. I've seen results on some White Pentecostal sisters that were near bald. I was so impressed. It can be purchased at most Wal-Marts salons.

Ok, you want good looking hair but now you are going to say, "I can't afford it." Right? My answer *(let me preach to you awhile).* We Pentecostal women do not buy jewelry, make-up and such, so I say, **buy the good shampoos and conditioners**. Spend the money and look great. We are God's women. Get your glory looking its best. You can't skimp on this one, girls. For the price of two boxes of kid's cereal you can buy good hair-care products.

Now we come to a very sensitive area. Hair Abuse. This seems to be a plight of many sisters. My research has supported the fact that many kinds of chemicals have damaged women's hair. Here is a testimony of a dear sister from the church in Dover, Delaware. Sister Chase entitled this *"Hair Today, Gone Tomorrow: Where did my hair go?"*

> *As a child my mom took care of my hair until I got married. I did go to the hairdresser for my engagement party and wedding—it was beautiful. After my wedding, my husband's military career took us to many different states. This was the start of many different hairdressers that began my hair problems. My first perm was my first burnout but because I was young it didn't all come out. It did however become very thin. I had one neighbor who did my hair with setting lotion and put me under a dryer and that was pretty good. My hair looked semi-pressed. Because the Air Force moved us to another state, I lost my contact with my neighbor. Another state...another hairdresser.*
>
> *Then we moved to England, and I had to show a hairdresser how to press my hair. By then, my husband*

was about ready to do my hair. Then we moved back to America, more perms year after year until one year my hair started falling out. There were bald spots on my head. I wore wigs, hats, or extensions. I was so embarrassed! When I went to church and worked in the kitchen I wore a scarf to hide my bad looking hair. One sister made me feel greatly at ease and comforted me about my hair. I was only to go back to perms again!

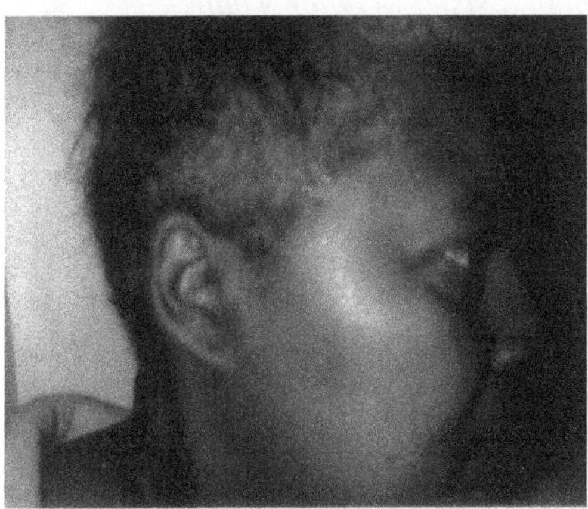

Sister Brenda Chase's fried hair

*This is when Sister Juli Jasinski came to visit our church. It was then I bought her book, "**My Hair, My Glory**." I learned that the Bible was very direct in no cutting your hair. I also heard other ladies in our church talking about what the Scripture teaches and how Sister Jasinski's book gave the reasons why not to cut your hair. I turned and asked many of these sisters to pray for me. I thought it was time to stop perming my hair because I knew it was damaging it. I decided to get extensions only to later have them taken out. I found another sister in the church and we became "hair-blessing" sisters. I blessed her hair and she blessed mine. In a short time my hair started growing out!*

The extensions needed to come out because as my hair grew out, they made my hair look like dred locks. I did not want that style, Praise the Lord. I was shocked that I had longer hair. I'm so grateful to Sister Jasinski's courage, care and concern enough to want to help a sister like me. She wanted to help a black sister with hair trouble. She was so excited to see that my hair had grown out. Her face was glowing. I never saw someone so enthused about a sister of color's hair.

May God bless her in all she does,
In the Name of Jesus
Sister Brenda Chase
Dover, Delaware

This testimony came unsolicited. And of course, I care about any sister whose hair is in need of help. This sister of color, Sister Chase, just latched on to the hair care tips and principles that were in both the books and God did the rest.

Another sister emailed me stating that when virgin hair is washed, it shrinks tremendously and becomes extremely curly and bushy. She says it's very difficult to manage. She states that the hair looks like the Afro styles of the '60s and this to her, looks masculine-like. This is why straightening or processing the hair provides more options for feminine styles. She would have me stress the difference between uncut hair and abused hair. The abuse comes when relaxers and perms are used to extreme measures and mix it with infrequent shampooing; you've got a mess.

I found numerous articles on the subject. A word of caution first: I was told that if I were to address these hair styling techniques that I'd "attempt to mock another race." Please be forewarned **I'm not mocking anybody**. This is what the pros say happen to hair when it is handled in this manner. I hope I'm clear on this point. It needs to be said that this continued practice only leads to damaged hair. And perhaps, you know this first-hand. I wonder, could this chemical onslaught be just another deviant plan of the devil?

Let's just be wise and not prolong the abuse, and grow some hair here. I felt that a good understanding of what these articles have discovered would only add to a good working knowledge to avoid further abuse. Remember the verse in Hosea 4:6 ***"My people are destroyed for lack of knowledge: because thou hast rejected knowledge, I will also reject thee."*** Let's hope this in not your case and learn this information.

Here are a few articles that I found. In an article, "Minerals in Hair of Healthy Black Children" published in the *Public Health Report* journal, September/October 1991, found that a normal child, whose hair had been treated with Vaseline, had excessively high lead and arsenic concentrations.[10] Furthermore, one of the most knowledgeable trichologists in the world, Philip Kinsley states in the article, "Treating Different Hair Types," found in March 1992 edition of *Vogue Magazine*, "straightening is the worst chemical process you can subject your hair to." "More damaging than a perm," he continues "because there's traction involved."[11]

Black hair is the most susceptible to damage and oddly, receives the most abuse. An estimated 75 percent of black women in America straighten their hair either chemically or with heat-styling tools. The reason for this type of hair to be especially sensitive to damage and abuse is because of its structure. The hair shaft is beaded rather than smooth (like a string of pearls) making the passage of natural oils from the scalp down the strand of hair to the ends is inhibited. Weak points run intermittently through each curl making it also difficult to brush.[12]

Hair breaks when it is dragged straight after each washing but more abuse is caused also with heat (hot irons) and pulling. Hair loss is inevitable around the face due to constant stretching and tugging. Cornrowing, like extensions and weaves, only compound the problem. Hairdressers tend to pull the hair tightly against the scalp to make styles last longer, which weakens the hair at the roots. Deep conditioning is the best way to build back elasticity and resilience to hair.[13]

Pearl Cleage, an Atlanta based writer, in her article "Hair Peace," published in *African American Review* Spring 1993, speaks about her experience as a child. She recalls the days in the kitchen where they did hair. She could distinctly remember how the hot grease felt when her mother wasn't paying attention and it dripped from the red-hot comb down onto her neck before she could catch it with the towel. It was lying nearby so her mother could test the heat of the comb every time she drew it out of the flame of the stove.[14] They have found that frequent use of hot combs is dangerous because of the burns to the neck and face areas and bald spots on the scalp. Most people think that slow growing hair (or non-growing hair) is hereditary –it is—only to say that the hair styling practices have been handed down traditionally in many homes of African American women.

"Much of the black hair fashion has caused much damage such as rashes, hair loss, acne or folliculitis" says Dr. Patricia Treadwell, associate professor of pediatrics and dermatology at Indiana University School of Medicine in Indianapolis in her article Dangers in African American Hair Styles printed in the *Ms Magazine*, July/August 1992. She states, "with braiding (plaiting and cornrowing), the constant twisting of the hair stresses the hair shafts and follicles, where new growth begins. If hair follicles become inflamed by the constant tension of braiding, hair loss—known as traumatic or traction alopecia—can occur. If the high-tension hairstyle is discontinued, the condition may be reversed.[15]

If the practice of hair pulling is not discontinued then the follicles may be permanently damaged and hair will cease from growing. In some cases, scar tissue is formed where follicles have been damaged and then also, stop producing hair. This is the primary reason for some female pattern of baldness.[16]

When one's hair is relaxed the cream used causes the chemical bonds of the hair shaft to break down, disrupting the elliptical shape and reconstructs the bonds in a different way. The hair can become dry and brittle and break off easily. Lye-based relaxers can cause scalp burns and sores. Pomades are waxy mixtures of oils, petroleum jelly, lanolin, or gums that get hair to stay in place. The continuous use may result in inflamed hair follicles, causing allergic reactions especially to the face.[17]

In a *FDA Consumer Report Magazine*, March 1996 I found an interesting article called, Hair Relaxers Destroyed after Consumers Complain. It stated two types of hair relaxers, valued at almost $2 million, were destroyed last fall after thousands of consumer reported problems with them. In 1994, and early 1995, more than 3,000 people reported to FDA that their scalp itched or burned and that hair broke off or fell out—and in some cases, turned green after using their product. The company later faced over 200 individual lawsuits.[18]

Author Lisa Jones, wrote in her book *Bulletproof Diva: tales of race, sex, and hair* that most of these hair-care products are owned by white manufactures. "*Viewpoint of Chicago* recently published a brand-awareness survey that showed black consumers were unpleasantly surprised and downright disturbed to find out that major black hair-care products such as African Pride, All Ways, TCB, Dark & Lovely, Right-On Curl, and Let's Jam are not made by black businesses." She stated that most of the $1.5 billion black hair-care industry in dominated by white-owned companies.[19]

Geri D. Jones, president of the American Health and Beauty Aids Institute (AHBAI) calls these companies "deceptive" in that white companies' use of Afrocentric marketing to black consumers. It leads people to believe that they are Black owned. Ninety-eight percent of the profit made from these product companies usually doesn't hire equally high numbers of black employees. However nowadays, she states, most consumers know which brands are black made and have shown a preference for these products in the future.[20]

Black Enterprise Magazine published a report in April

1995, stating black hair care has become a very lucrative business. In fact, the ethnic total of the health and beauty aids industry (hair, skin and cosmetic products and services) rakes in over $2.8 billion a year![21] Yikes! Later the magazine reported in their March 1997 edition in an article "A Hair-raising Success" that smart promotions of products via magazines exceeded companies revenues to an estimated $1.5 million.[22] *I guess you can say that advertising works.*

The marketing and advertising industry not only reaches to capture the black audience but also the naïve white girls looking for the latest fashions. In *Vogue Magazine,* November 1995, editor Amy Astley wrote an article entitled "Getting it Straight." She states that the alchemy of turning curly hair into straight has been a three-decade feat.[23] No matter how risky the method, no matter how slim the promise, her and her sisters were in pursuit of a super-straight fashion. Relaxing it, ironing it wrapping it, blowing it, stretching it around giant rollers (the bigger, the better, she says), sitting for hours under a hair dryer with cotton shielding her red, red ears[24]...they had to get it straight.

The methods were drastic if not down right, silly. She states most products have chemicals that penetrate the cuticle of the hair and open it up as they raise the pH level of hair. If the product is too high, between ten and twelve, the cuticle might burst, resulting in utterly fried hair that can break off in your hand. *(In the olden days they used to call them "pocket perms" because when the hair broke off the hairdresser used to hide the hair in his pocket.)* What a price for beauty...it's no wonder the Proverb says "beauty is vain." The dictionary declares the meaning of **vain** as: "Not yielding the desired outcome." Vain is right; it all adds up to nothing!

In conclusion, let's forever dissolve all the antiquated stereotypical hype about what is "good" hair and what is "bad." The fact is, everyone has good hair—you just have to know how to take care of it. The Lord is reaching for you to once again stop fighting against it and call a truce. Be at peace with what God has given you. Your beauty touches the heart. Your beauty touches *my* heart…and God's.

---

[1] Ayana Byrd & Lori Tharps, *Hair History: Untangling the Roots of Black Hair in America,* (New York: St. Martin's Press, 2000) p148.
[2] Ibid, p149.
[3] Lonnice Brittenum Bonner, *Good Hair*, (New York: Three Rivers Press, 1990) p18.
[4] Ibid.
[5] Pamela Ferrell, *Where Beauty Touches Me*, (Washington, DC: Cornrows & Co Publication, 1993) p9.
[6] Ibid, p16.
[7] Andre Walker, *Andre Talks Hair,* (New York: Simon & Schuster, 1997) p11-12.
[8] Ibid.
[9] *Heart & Soul Magazine,* Editors, Looking Good Naturally, (Emmaus: Rodale Press, Inc. 1996) p24-25.
[10] *Public Health Reports*, Theresa B. Haddy, MD, Minerals in Hair of Health Black Children, September/October 1991, Vol. 106, No. 5, p560.
[11] *Vogue Magazine,* Treating Different Hair Types, March 1992, p256.
[12] Ibid.
[13] Ibid.
[14] *African American Review,* Pearl Cleage, Hair Peace, Spring 1993, Vol. 27, n1, p39.
[15] *Ms Magazine*, Dangers in African American Hair Styles, editors, July/August 1992, p39.
[16] Pamela Ferrell, Where Beauty Touches Me, (Washington, DC: Cornrows & Co Publication, 1993) p40.

[17] Ibid.

[18] FDA Consumer Report Magazine, Hair Relaxers Destroyed after Consumers Complain, editors, March 1996, p33.
[19] Lisa Jones, *Bulletproof Diva: tales of race, sex, and hair,* (New York: Double Day, 1993) p301.
[20] Ibid.
[21] *Black Enterprise Magazine,* Enterprise, editors, April 1995, p31.
[22] *Black Enterprise Magazine,* Enterprise, editors, March 1997, p32.
[23] *Vogue Magazine,* Amy Astley, Getting it Straight, November 1995, p249.
[24] Ibid.

Diagram Credits:

Diagram 1—John Dalton, *Professional Cosmetologist.*
Diagram 2—Pamela Ferrell, *Where Beauty Touches Me*, p9.

Chapter 12

Answering the Tough Questions

Throughout my travels teaching "Hair Seminars," I'm always, without a doubt, asked the tough questions. "What about the add-ons," they inquire, "you know, **Veils, Hats and other coverings**?" Knowing that these legitimate questions can't be ignored; I just could not give a blanket answer...well then you say, what about them? Are they wrong or are they okay?

Each of these add-ons has history of itself and came into being for some reason. Searching for logical answers on these subjects this is what I've found. Before we begin let's look again at the Scripture text,

First Corinthians, chapter 11:4-7 & 13-16

1CO 11:4 Every man praying or prophesying, having his head covered, dishonoureth his head.
1CO 11:5 But every woman that prayeth or prophesieth with her head uncovered dishonoureth her head: for that is even all one as if she were shaven.
1CO 11:6 For if the woman be not covered, let her also be shorn: but if it be a shame for a woman to be shorn or shaven, let her be covered.
1CO 11:7 For a man indeed ought not to cover his

(Verse 8-12 we discussed in chapter 1)
1CO 11:10 For this cause ought the woman to have power on her head because of the angels.
Skip verse 11-12
1CO 11:13 Judge in yourselves: is it comely that a woman pray unto God uncovered?
1CO 11:14 Doth not even nature itself teach you, that, if a man have long hair, it is a shame unto him?
1CO 11:15 But if a woman have long hair, it is a glory to her: for her hair is given her for a covering.

Covering

It is interesting to note that Paul mentions the woman's hair and angels as an interconnecting function. ***1Corinthians 11:10 " For this cause ought the woman to have power on her head because of the angels."*** She ought to (Greek indicates obligation) have power because of the angels. Why is this? There have been many thoughts surmised on this verse. To whatever degree, the one I hold to is in her obedience to God's Word. It makes her a powerful praying tool in God's hand should she wear her symbol of submission (uncut hair).

Jesus Christ was our prime example of gaining much power through his obedience to the cross. Obedience also becomes an outward sign of submission and has power in and of itself *(For a complete explanation of the relationship of angels and a woman's hair see **My Hair, My Glory**)*. The woman's uncut hair is a covering that has angels stationed nearby for her beckoning call.

The only other place the Bible mentions a covering with angels is the Ark of the Covenant. This was the piece of furniture located in the Holiest of Holy in the Tabernacle, which housed the presence of the Lord. This was the place where God met Moses and the preceding High Priests.

The box itself was made of acacia wood overlaid with fine pure gold. Its lid, called the mercy seat, was the place where sins were covered. The lid interestingly had two angels (cherubims) facing each other and fashioned together (Ex 37:7). Hence, the covering and angels were one piece.

The cherubim looked down upon the bloodstained Mercy Seat, acquiescing and admiring. They symbolized the power of God in creation and providence. They were the revelation to God's people of the holy presence and unapproachableness of God, and at the same time, they were the holy royal guard of the Divine Majesty of the Lord.[1]

The Mercy Seat represented a throne or a dwelling place here on earth for the Almighty God. And the angels were the protectors of the holiness of the Most High. The cherubims also symbolized the eternal watchfulness and ministry of the redeemed and their co-operation with God in the plan of redemption (He 1:14).

Now through Jesus Christ, we can go into the Holy of Holiest and make our petitions known. We can boldly approach the throne (He 4:16; 9: 8-28; 10:16-20). We have this right through the blood of Jesus Christ as we take on his name in baptism and receive the baptism of the Holy Ghost. Amen!

It is awesome to know we have this privilege. God's mercy was on his blood stained covering. Our hair is our covering of God's mercy. It's frightening to consider however, if a woman knowingly, yet so flippantly, cut her glory (remove God's power, providence, and protection) and <u>think</u> it doesn't matter. She really doesn't quite grasp God's holiness. How many women perhaps reap a whirlwind of trouble by not obeying this awesome truth?

Just as the Shechinah glory of the Lord overshadowed the Mercy Seat as was witnessed by the High Priest, we too, are the temples (tabernacle) of the Lord with the indwelling Holy Spirit of God. The cheribums hovered as to guard the glory of God. Their presence intermingled with God's presence was visibly manifested in a cloudy pillar and fire. The glorious light of God's presence enveloped the tabernacle in a cloud and burst forth at times.

The power of Christ overshadows the believers as well, as in this antitype of the Old Testament. Hence, angels encamped around the children of Israel as the angels encircle God's holy women today. When we honor this God-given principle we invite the glory of God into our lives. And you will receive all of his power.

It is exceedingly important for Holy Ghost-filled women not to cut off this glory. As we wear this symbol of glory on our head we in turn are honoring His glory. When we cut off this symbol with a mere snip of the shears, cut of the scissors, or lop of our tresses just as if it were nothing, the glory of the Lord departs from us.

Even if we don't necessarily **cut** our hair but we *tamper with* our glory (hair) as to interrupt the growth or hinder it from being in its God-given state, this results in a great stifling of the flow of God's presence in our life. Thus, we must walk circumspectly in this life and be careful as to how we handle it.[2]

Uncovered Head

In many commentaries, scholars seem to stress the fact that an unveiled woman shows her impropriety in the public assemblies. These writers put extra emphasis on the veil showing the woman's subjection to the man. Charles Hodge in his *Exposition of First Corinthians* writes, "The veil in all eastern countries was and to a great extent still is, the symbol of modesty and subjection." Hodge declares that for a woman to discard the veil was to be immodest and show her refusal to recognize her subordination to her husband.[3]

One comes away with a strong sense that the emphasis was put on the woman just to conform to this position of subordination, almost in a tyrannical way. While the Spirit of the Lord wanted each of us to submit one to another, I don't believe it was in such a despotic manner. After studying their writings, one is left with the feeling that the woman was the only one who was to submit.

There are numerous examples of submission recorded in the Bible. For example: we are told to **subject ourselves one to another** and to **elders** 1Pe 5:5, to the **law** and **ordinances** 1Pe 2:13, to **God** James 4:7, to **those who have the rule over you** Heb 13:17, to the **Gospel** 2 Co 9:13, and to the **Father** Heb 12:9. Children are to be **subject to parents** 1Ti 2:4, and we are to **keep our body in subjection** 1Co 9:27 and finally, **wives to their husbands** 1Pe 3:1, 5. Hence, all Christians are to submit.

John Welsey founder of the Methodist Church (1738), wrote in his commentary, *Notes of the Whole Bible*, "a man who prays or prophesies with a veil on his head, reflects a dishonor on Christ, whose representative he is." He continues to exhorts his readers in verse six by saying, if a woman be not covered "for it is the same, in effect, as if [the woman] cut her hair short, and wore it in the distinguishing form of the men."[4]

Adam Clarke's Commentary (1810-1826) states that if a man has his head covered, that is, wearing his **cap** or **turban**, dishonors his head; because the head being covered was a sign of subjection. And while he was employed in the public ministration of the word, he was to be considered as a representative of Christ.

On this account his [the man] being veiled or covered would be improper. When Paul the apostle made these statements in his letter, it was seen as point blank hostility to the canons of the Jews. *(Perhaps he knew the Jews would be reading this epistle).* It is interesting to note that Jewish law would not allow a man to pray unless he was veiled [or wearing a *yarmulke {dome-shape beanie}*]. Let's take a side trip and learn its history.

The very ancient custom of wearing *yarmulkes* (head-coverings) has become an accepted practice among Jews for centuries. The Talmud (Babylonian edition 200BCE-427CE) tells a story of a rabbi who ate fruit that wasn't his. He blamed his error on the fact that he didn't have a head covering on to remind him of heaven above; thus, the wearing of the cap was started to be that reminder. The word "*yarmulka*" comes from the Aramaic "*Yarei Malka*," Fear of the King.

One who wears a *yarmulka,* it is said, believes that there is a Higher Power to be accountable to. It's their symbol of humility and submission to the Divine. This was a practice continued for hundreds of years. The Chassidic Jews wear two coverings (cap and hat) representing two surrounding elements of the soul.[5]

So the fact that Paul didn't want converted Christian men to wear a covering (cap, hat or veil) meant total surrender to God under the New Testament covenant. Remember that sin ruined the man's image for he was created in the image of God. Up to this point, Jewish men, and perhaps men in general, covered their head with some type of covering. His uncovered head meant he was agreeing to the principle of reflecting the image of Christ as God. He was saying in essence, "Yes, I fully believe that Jesus is Messiah, God in the flesh and I submit to Him and this truth."

The disregarding of a covering or wearing a cap gave the traditional Jews one more thing to fight against.

Veils

Throughout the ages these few verses have become quite controversial yet, archaeologists have found evidence in art dating back to Paul's century that depicts women's head coverings and hairstyles. Most of the statues that survived seem to be that of upper class Greco-Roman women. Studying the pictures of these statues will aid us to understand his comments to the Christian Corinthian women. We could note undoubtedly that many women did wear some type of head covering but not necessarily in a church setting.

Some scholars believe Paul was not talking about veils at all. Bible scholar Cynthia L. Thompson contends that Paul may have not been referring to veils but hairstyles.[6] In worship, female prophets were to wear long hair fastened up instead of flowing down. Thus, their pinned up hair (not veils) was to be their head covering.

Elisabeth Schüssler Fiorenza, in her book, *In Memory of Her: A Feminist Theological Reconstruction of Christian Origins* states that the pagan worshipers of Isis would worship with unbound hair. She suggests that Paul didn't want Christian women to leave the "impression of madness and frenzy so typical of orgiastic cultic worship" and they must therefore project a more proper image with restrained hairstyles.[7]

The practice of women letting their hair fly wildly and uncovered was associated with pagan rituals. For example, in worshipping Dionysus, god of wine and revelry, women let their hair fly loose like "mythic Maenads." Maenads were female worshippers of Dionysus and usually depicted in mythology as "madwomen." This is where the English word "maniac" comes from. "Maenads" has its roots similar in Latin and Greek.[8]

Now let's read the scripture in this perspective that a woman should keep her hair long and restrained. *This is my paraphrase,*

First Corinthians, chapter 11:4-7 & 13-16

1CO 11:4 Every man praying or prophesying, having his head covered (excessive hair)**, dishonoureth his head** (Christ)**.**
1CO 11:5 But every woman that prayeth or prophesieth with her head uncovered (hair unrestrained; not pinned back and up) **dishonoureth her head** (husband; and for unmarrieds; God, Isa. 54:5): **for that** (disheveled hair) **is even all one** (the same thing) **as if she were shaven.**
1CO 11:6 For if the woman be not covered (hair not restrained; not pinned back and up), ***let her also be shorn: but if it be a shame for a woman to be shorn or shaven, let her be covered*** (hair restrained; pinned back and up).
1CO 11:7 For a man indeed ought not to cover his head (with excessive hair), **forasmuch as he is the image and glory of God: but the woman is the glory of the man.**

1CO 11:13 Judge in yourselves: is it comely (Grk: to tower up, implying, to be suitable, or proper) **that a woman pray unto God uncovered** (with hair unrestrained, not pinned back and up)? **My paraphrase:**

you judge, is your hair towered up (proper) when it's hanging down?

1CO 11:14 Doth not even nature itself teach you, that, if a man have long hair, it is a shame unto him?

1CO 11:15 But if a woman have long hair, it is a glory to her: for her hair is given her for a covering.

Paul may have not wanted the Gentile Christian female prophets wearing unrestrained hair. In one traditional Jewish view, during this time and still believed, loose hair was a sign of **uncleanness**. Proper Jewish women wore their hair pinned up and out of harm's way of touching that, which is unclean. And we know from the Law that uncleanness, *tumah*, would be a grave offense. Thus, one must avoid all that makes you unclean in order to maintain true holiness.

One Jewish friend told me she believed it was because of sanitary reasons when women prepared meat and food products. According to rabbinic teaching, "forbidden food, for example, contaminates the soul, that is, keeps a person far from the divine."[9] So Paul may have been saying this chidingly when he said, "hair down (uncovered) is as disgraceful as shaving hair off like a man" (my paraphrase).

Back to veils.

I've found that in the house of Vesta, six virgin priestesses who guarded the hearth to ensure Rome's prosperity were shown wearing veils. In *Metamorphosis*, Lucius Apuleius, a second century Roman writer mentioned that women wore veils when worshipping the Egyptian goddess Isis near Corinth.[10]

It is interesting to note, men, as well as women, wore head coverings in their culture. For example, this art shows a woman and two men sacrificing at the "Altar of the Lares" (Altar of the gods). Lares were Roman protector gods of households, associations (communities of worship), and cities.[11] The custom of the dominant Greco-Roman peoples was that veils were worn in religious functions (sacrificing).

Let's look at the origin of veils and how they came into being. It's important to point out that nowhere in the Old Testament, as far as I can tell, was it mandated for a woman to wear a veil on her head. However, the first mention of a veil in the Bible is when Rebecca covered her self upon sighting her intended husband, Issac from afar (Gen. 24:65). So where did the custom come from?

We know first of all, the Bible refers to hair as an ornament enhancing the appearance of a woman. It's her glory. A woman's long hair embellishes her. For example, King Solomon expresses this on his wedding night to his Shulamite bride (Song of Solomon 4:1, 6:5). In later writings, Jewish rabbis recorded in the Talmud that a woman's long hair is regarded not only as beautiful but erotic and for that reason it had to be covered.

Leila Bronner, professor of Jewish History at the University of Judaism, states in her article, *From Veil to Wig: Jewish Women's Hair Covering*, "the Mishnah appears to say that the duty to cover hair is a *dat Yehudit,* rather than a 'Law of Moses.'" She continues, "clearly implying that there is a distinction between a 'Mosaic Law' and 'Jewish Law' (*dat Yehudit).* 'Mosaic Law' is apparently considered by the Mishnah to be Torah-derived, whereas 'Jewish Law' seems to be Jewish practice stemming from the people."[12] A continued practice of this sort is usually then considered a *custom.* Thus, a custom is formulated by the practice of the people and often receives the force of law, not decreed from on high by authorities.

The Midrash implicitly teaches that Eve used her

attractiveness [hair] to seduce Adam into sin. Consequently, it became the woman's responsibility to modestly cover her hair because this part of her body's alluring feature made men to be powerless to resist. (*Time Out!..this is only speculation here because ain't nobody got the truth as to what exactly happen in the garden that day).* However, this Jewish custom of female modesty became law. And was so severe that if she was caught with her hair unbound and uncovered in public her husband could divorce her without benefit of compensatory financial support.[13] (*Yikes!)*

The customary laws were interestingly only in connection with women's behavior. (A rabbi said it's because the female is most attractive). Modesty laws in rabbinic literature acted to render the woman inaccessible and unavailable to all but her husband. Rouselle, a cultural historian, writes in regard to ancient Rome that the veil or hood worn by an honorable woman "constituted a warning: It signified that the wearer was a respectable woman and that no man dares approach without risking grave penalties. Although the veil was a symbol of subjection, it was also a badge of honor, of sexual reserve, and hence of mastery of the self."

Rouselle continues saying that it not only showed the woman's modesty but also of the wife belonging to a particular man and the veil had to be worn whenever she was in mixed company or went out in public.[14] Interestingly, in Jewish tradition, they believe that because "women are on a higher spiritual level than men, they [women] don't need a reminder that there is a Higher Being as the Jewish men do. Therefore the Law says unmarried women and girls do not wear head coverings![15]

Rabbi Silberberg says that women's hair is sensuous. Once a woman is married, she should cover her hair (Talmud Ketubot 72a, Bamidbar 5:18). She reserves her sensuous side for her husband only, thus, not "advertising" her sensuality.[16]

This custom was not only strong amongst the people of

Israel but also many other Middle East nations. One only has to dive into anthropology to find a cross-cultural study of hair coverings. It had great symbolism in the Muslim countries. The findings are quite shocking. Carol Delaney of Stanford University observed this eye-opening behavior.

After twenty months living in Turkey, she was able to ask questions regarding the significance of female hair and the wearing of veils. Delaney recalled one Muslim scholar, Bouhdiba saying, "there is an undeniable fetishism of hair in Islam, the significance of which is both sexual and religious." She informs us that throughout Islam countries, hair has a strong symbol of the relationship of sexuality intertwined with religion.[17]

She witnessed that in the country of Turkey, long hair is both the glory and symbol of womanhood. Women are thought to have a loose and rampant sexuality, and must be tamed and brought under control. The braiding of the bride-to-be's hair on her wedding day symbolized her coming under that control. (*I always wondered why I saw a single braid down the back of married Muslim women).* The braiding was followed by their customary removal of all body hair. Women then are expected to comply strictly with this practice [body hair removal] throughout their lives.

Delaney's study shows that female hair not only has sexual significance but characteristically seen as phallic. "Very commonly head hair becomes the focus of ritual attention because the head is being used as a symbol for the phallus and hair as a symbol for semen."[18] Thus we can deduce then that the woman is seen as a mere sex object that a man can have his way with.

In Turkey according to Delaney, there is a phallocentric bias that has been challenged by few. Puberty for a girl meant it was time to put the headscarf on and she was soon to be married. Brides were as young as thirteen years of age. Islamic dress known in the Arab world as *hijab* is believed to remove women from being perceived as erotic and sexual objects.

Up to this time in our study of veils, we saw that during Paul's day and time past [Issac's day] that the veil only covered the top of the head. In the Middle East however, women are made to cover their mouth, forehead, ears, and in some pictures I've seen, they were covered completely with only a tiny screen for the eyes.

Women's hair comes to symbolize, Delaney discovers the physical entanglements by which men are ensnared and thus must be kept out of sight. The sight of women's hair, it is believed, to trigger uncontrollable sexual desires in men, perhaps because of the connection with the phallus, head hair and female genitals. (*Now, we know the truth why they veil their women).*

During the duration of Delaney's anthropological research, many Turkish men told her, "a woman's hair is the ruination of families." She says it's believed that not only a woman with uncovered hair would arouse a married man and cause him to commit adultery at least in his mind, but also that even within the house too much loose hair creates disturbance [distraction].[19] *One wonders where is the restraint and self-control of these men? And why are they so compulsive?*

Moreover Delaney states that in Muslim scholarly texts it declares that woman's hair may evoke the image of Sirat, the bridge over which souls of the dead must walk. It is said that the thickness of only one strand of hair slices the wicked like a razor and they fall into hell. The more pious men avow that for every strand of hair that a woman shows, she is said to burn one day in hell.[20]

Delaney finds that there is a strong symbol [hair] in the relationship of sexuality and religion cross-culturally. Specifically, in Hindus ascetics and Buddhist monks, for example—one lets the hair grow so that it becomes matted (supposedly indicating letting go of sexuality) while the other shaves their hair off completely (to indicate cutting off sexual life for religious ends).[21]

Jeannette Marie Mageo writes in her article "Hairdos and

Don'ts: Hair Symbolism and Sexual History in Samoa," found in *Man Magazine,* June 1994 that Samoan hair was a symbol of fecundity [fertility]. They too, believe "the long hair of female spirits is analogous [similar] to the penises of chiefs. As chiefs have remarkable genitals, female spirits have remarkable hair."[22]

So again we see a connection of hair and sexual innuendoes. Interestingly, the Samoan and Polynesian women are not necessarily required to wear veils, but they are obliged by parents to wear their long hair pinned back and up. If she walks in the village with dishevelled hair showing social discomposure, she is deprived of status altogether. Mageo states, a remark will be made of a girl who wears her hair down in the village, "look at the hanging of her hair, she is probably a wanton."[23] Most women keep their hair hidden in a bun.

Among the Polynesians of the Pacific, the first time a boy's hair was cut marked his coming of age. It was also a way in which he was now differentiated from women. Hair was thought to contain the *mana* or power, and so the cutting of hair was risky business.[24]

In the book, *African Women: Three Generations*, Mark Mathabane states that the normal age to be married for a girl was fifteen or sixteen, and some as young as twelve. When a girl becomes a woman by means of menstruating she then was soon sent to ritual school to learn their role in traditional society. The school taught them to accept polygamy in men, to obey them unconditionally, and to view their life as primarily one of sacrifice and self-denial.[25]

The groups of men often waited outside ritual schools to have their pick of the *tikhomba* (new-initiated). The girls were decked out in spectacular outfits, wearing veils to show they were prospective brides. *Sounds like a cattle market says the author*. The wearing of *doeks* (veils or headscarves) was to signify that the girls became completed women after a few months of training. After she became a wife, the woman would normally keep her hair shaved and hidden under her scarf.

The ideal of beauty was not so much the woman's hair but was her tallness, strong limbs, and large breasts, which was considered proof that the girl could have no trouble suckling strong children. A father could demand more *lobola* (money) simply on the basis of the size of his daughter's breasts. Among most villages, married women were soon involved with petty rivalries and jealousies to keep the attention of men.[26]

By this cross-cultural study of anthropology in the countries of Israel, Turkey, Somoa, and in Africa, we find that there was a significant amount of women in these cultures wearing head coverings. We learned that not only the women wore veils but also the men wore and still do wear caps, turbans or hats.

What is sometimes forgotten is that, until fairly recently, women in the West (USA) wore hats when they went out publicly and always covered their heads upon entering church. Up until around 1964, when Vatican II happened, the women covered their heads with a veil during Mass while women in Protestant churches covered theirs with hats.

Hats

The history of hats is not quite as complex as the veils yet they do have a bit of controversy. There are some people who hold that a woman is to wear a hat upon entering church, this may be a throw back from when in history women were required to wear something on their head. Some believe in the "doctrine of the second covering." There is no place in the Bible that teaches a second covering doctrine.

I've discovered in my searching that in some Apostolic Pentecostal churches women wear the veil but cut the hair under it. To my amazement, I learned that these women believe just because they wear a veil in church they have the right to cut their glory off! This is inherently wrong. They say we wear a veil so we can cut our hair. This is a gross misapplication of these scriptures. Nothing ever man-made can take the place of God-given glory.

Remember the children of Israel were carrying the Ark of the Covenant on an ox cart? This was not pleasing to the Lord. He gave strict instructions the Ark was to be carried by the priests. But Israel was not walking as close to God as before. They didn't read it in the Book as to HOW the Ark was to be carried. So they perhaps thought they could handle God's glory in any 'ol way. Uzzah reached out to touch it. That was all God could stand. God smote him for touching it.

We can never carry the glory of the Lord under something man-made and expect God to be pleased. It wasn't until David read in the Book how God's glory (Ark) was to be carried in order for his effort to please God. We can never think that we can transfer what God has called glory (our hair) to something man-made such as hats, veils or add-ons such as wigs, weaves, braids, or extensions. Let's be careful to stay in the Book and live by it. God's word says that our hair is our glory. He hasn't changed his mind on that one. Hats, veils and the add-ons are not glory. (*This doesn't mean we can't wear a hat at all, ever. It does mean that it's not deemed by God as glory).*

The history of hats is interesting. One of the first hats was found etched on a tomb painting at Thebes, Ancient City of Upper Egypt on the Nile River. Other early hats include the Pileus, which was a simple skullcap. It later became identified as the "liberty cap" given to slaves in Greece and Rome when they were made free men. The first hat with a brim comes from ancient Greece and is known as the *Pestasos*.

Women, we learned previously, were to keep their heads covered by veils, hoods, caps or wimples. It wasn't until the end of the 16th century women began being seen in structured hats, based on those worn by male courtiers.

The first record of hat making was in 1529. The word "milliner" was used as a maker of women's hats. The term referred to the products shipped from Milan and the northern Italian regions. The haberdashers (lit. petty wares) imported the popular straw, which the hats were made from; hence they were called "milliners."[27]

By the seventeenth century women's headgear began to emerge quite rapidly. By the mid 1800's Swiss and Italian straws mixed with imitation straws, grass and horsehair were available to women along with the introduction of velvet and tulle. During the first half of the nineteenth century the bonnet dominated the woman's fashion. Many were dressed up with ribbons, flowers and feathers. Even though the bonnet remained, the introduction of wide brim hats appeared on the scene. By the early 1900's most of the women's hats were enormous.

The nonsensical term "mad as a hatter" is said to of come out of the poisonous chemicals used as preservatives by hatters to cure the feathers from the brilliantly plumed humming birds, for the fashionable Edwardian women ladies. The chemicals induced convulsions along with other symptoms. Thus, the saying came to being.[28]

When hair cutting became vogue (1920's) the hats shrunk in design, and hugged the head like a helmet with a very small brim. From the 1930's to the 1950's the tendency for hats were to have higher crowns with smaller brims. The invention of ready-to-wear clothes nearly put the milliners out of business. And during the WWII, women were to busy working and no longer had much time or energy to spend on being fashionable.[29]

After the war with the rebuilding of Europe the hat remained but was slowly being replaced by wigs. In the 60's the hat was fully overtaken by hairdressers who colored, backcombed and sprayed women's hair into sculptures. Hats have never really recovered as fashion, only for special occasions. Princess Di's enthusiasm for wearing hats revived the market for hats but it too was short lived. Hats nowadays, have long since seen its day as a status symbol. Most hats are just used in uniforms, worn as protective headgear and collected as sports memorabilia.

Hats to the African American woman are a different story. They are of course, a way of life all by itself. In the book, *Crowns: Portraits of Black Women in Church Hats,* authors Michael Cunningham and Craig Marberry were intrigued by many hat-wearing African American queens. It is said that the hats these women wore are their crowns. The hat, was in essence, a transfer of their natural glory (hair) to that of the hat. Thus, the hat became their glory.

Many women recorded in *Crowns* believe that the Bible says for a woman to cover their head so for them hats are not mere fashion accessories. Marberry states, "Church hats are a peculiar convergence of faith and fashion that keeps the Sabbath both holy and glamorous."[30]

He interviewed a wide range of ladies from various black denominations *(none from the Apostolic faith, however)* to learn their stories. Some own as few as three hats while others as many as 350. Many ladies loved hats while few really hated them. One lady mentioned she was a minister's wife and felt it was her duty to wear a hat and with it she believed that the Bible taught her to adorn herself well and never cut her hair.

Another lady had the flip side of that story. She keeps her

hair cut short and wears a tam instead of a hat. She believed hats were made for those bad-hair days. She goes on to describe that when her hair is short-short, she said the hat itself makes her look like a boy.

Ms. Brown said about the same thing. She said that over a period of time, her hair turned so brittle, short, and uneven. So wearing a hat, she exclaimed, could hide the mess. People would tell her that if she kept cutting it, it would thicken but it never did. She wondered what was wrong. So finally, her grandmother told her she needed to find a hairdresser with "a growing hand."

The old folks believe that some people have the touch; they can touch your hair and automatically it will grow. When she found a hairdresser, Torina, she pulled off the scarf she wore at the salon. Torina said it was those cheap hats that Ms. Brown wore. Her hairdresser said wool damages permed hair. A perm is a chemical relaxer, and chemicals and wool just don't mix. She said hats are less harmful if they are lined with silk. Her advice: if you've got a perm, ditch the wool. It's not your nerves; it's your hats!

Ms. Easter said that she wishes black women would wear more conservative hats. You shouldn't wear anything that is going to block the view of someone sitting behind you in church. She didn't like gaudy hats. She also commented that if it weren't for the black women, the hat industry would be out of business.

Ms. Graves says when a COGIC woman walks into church with a hat; she walks in with an attitude. Ms. Guion says any woman can just plop a hat on their head, but they can't carry it off until they have an attitude to go with it. She calls it "hattitude." Another lady says, "listen, never touch my hat." She claims there is a special way you are to hug a lady with a hat on. Be careful, those are her "hat-queen rules."

"African American women dress to the nines to go to church. It's part of their heritage. Church was the only time slaves were allowed to congregate so if they had something to show off and be in style, you'd wear it to church," says Ms.

Jenkins. In an article I found in *Charisma Magazine*, "The Tops in Sunday Fashion" April 1997, Valerie G. Lowe states the (COGIC) women report a great increase in compliments when wearing a pretty hat as well as quicker service and better seats in a restaurant. Milliner Jack McConnell notes that the COGIC convention in Tennessee is a hat-affair each year. He creates one-of-a-kind hats for COGIC women that cost as much as $1,000. Department hats range from $35.00 to $250.00. *That seems pretty pricey just to get a compliment.*

However, Ms. Manigault believes according to *Crowns* that when a person goes to church to present yourself before God, who is excellent and holy, there should be excellence in all things, including your appearance. We should not be dressed too casual says Ms. Lewis, when we go to church. She doesn't believe in wearing pants or anything too informal. She points out that in England, women wear hats all the time, the royals and the regular folks. So women should dress up and wear their hat like a queen.

Finally, my favorite, Ms. Gaither, says when the spirit is moving in her Holiness church, the congregates make some noise. And she rightly has a good time in the Lord. When she gets to preach'n the hat usually flies in one direction and her feet in another. *(Sounds like she's having church).* She has never let a pretty hat inhibit her from receiving a blessing.[31]

Now in the next chapter we'll discuss the history of Wigs, Braids, Extensions & Weaves.

[1] John Ritchie, The Tabernacle in the Wilderness, (Grand Rapids: Kregel Publications, 1982) p110-111.
[2] Linda Reed, *Guardians of His Glory*, CD ROM
[3] Charles Hodge, *Exposition of First Corinthians,* p227 (Ages Digital Library Commentary CD ROM).
[4] John Welsey, *Notes of the Whole Bible,* NT I Corinthians, p544 (Ages Digital Library Commentary CD ROM).
[5] Rabbi N. Silberberg, *AskMoses.com*
[6] Cynthia L. Thompson, "Hairstyles, Head-coverings and St. Paul: Portraits from Roman Corinth," *Biblical Archeologist*, June 1988, p112.
[7] Elisabeth Schüssler Fiorenza, *In Memory of Her: A Feminist Theological Reconstruction of Christian Origins,* (New York: Crossroad, 1989), p230.
[8] Ibid
[9] Louis Jacobs, *The Book of Jewish Belief*, (New Jersey: Behrman House, Inc. 1984) p199.
[10] Ibid
[11] Nancy A. Carter, *Paul and Corinthian Women's Head Coverings.*
[12] Leila Bronne, *From Veil to Wig: Jewish Women's Hair Covering,* p467.
[13] Ibid
[14] Ibid.
[15] Rabbi N. Silberberg, *AskMoses.com*
[16] Ibid
[17] Carol Delaney, "Untangling the Meanings of Hair in Turkish Society," *Anthropological Quarterly*, October 1994, Vol. 67, n4, p159.
[18] Ibid, p162.
[19] Ibid, p165.
[20] Ibid
[21] Ibid, p162.
[22] Jeannette Marie Mageo, "Hairdos and Don'ts: Hair Symbolism and Sexual History in Samoa," *Man Magazine,* June 1994, p411.
[23] Ibid, p419.
[24] Eras of Elegance, *A Brief History of Hairstyles*, www.eraofelegance.com
[25] Mark Mathabane, *African Women: Three Generations,* (Harper Collins Publishers, 1994) p213.
[26] Ibid, p29.
[27] "History of Hats," The Hat Bible, www.hatsuk.com
[28] Angela Pidduck, "The Hat in History," www.sputnick.com
[29] Ibid
[30] Michael Cunningham and Craig Marberry, *Crowns: Portraits of Black Women in Church Hats,* (New York: Doubleday, 2000) p4.
[31] Ibid p22,26,43,47,70,75,91,106,131,162,179.

Chapter 13

More Answers

Wigs

What about wearing wigs, braids, weaves or extensions? Here are some more answers. First of all, there is plenty of history on wigs. We know the wearing of wigs date as far back as 3000 BC. Both Egyptian men and women shaved their heads and wore wigs. Some say it was not only for personal adornment but also was to protect them from the fierce heat of the desert. Other people groups such as the Assyrians, Phoenicians, Greeks and Romans were noted at times to have worn wigs.

During each different time periods, with each dynasty came different wig fashions, hence, wigs were dressed in many different ways. Generally speaking, the hair became longer and more complicated with an arrangement of curls and braids—set in beeswax. In addition, early records indicate that some of the Egyptians wore semicircular kerchiefs, tied by the corners at the nape of the neck under the hair, to protect the wig from dusty days.

It is not until the 16th century however; the wig became big in fashion. During the reign of Queen Elizabeth I, the men wore the periwigs. This was the first trend since ancient Egypt wore her wigs. This became the norm for over one hundred years and especially when King Louis XIII, began wearing wigs in 1624.

France established the industry in 1665, with the formation of the wig maker's guild. Thus the wig became a distinctive class symbol as part of an official costume—some legal systems still wear wigs in courts today.

Braids

Now let's look at the interesting history of the braid. According to one historian, Rodrick Owen, braids were a symbol of power, valued adjuncts to ritual and ceremony and imbued with meaning. W. L. Hilburgh, writing in 1944, noted that, "When a family was afraid of witchery, they would undertake some kind of *lavori intereaciati* (braided work)."

"For witches cannot enter a house," states Hilburgh, "where there is anything of the kind hung up—so in making garments of any kind for men or women, they should include interlaced braids or stitches. For when the witches see such interlacing they can do nothing because they cannot count the threads nor stitches."[1]

It is not concluded that hair braids have the same type of association of the previous mentioned superstitions. In some Native American beliefs it says that the three-strand hair braid represents the intertwining of the body, the spirit and the mind.[2]

As far back as 3500 B.C., braids were worn by Ancient Egyptian women in their natural hair and in the form of wigs. Folds, braids, and curly tresses were a source of pride for women of the East. Thus, they always paid special attention to their hair.[3] Most of the extensions and wigs during this time were made from real hair or sheep's wool.

In many countries in Africa, especially among the Temne people, they believed the fine braided rows on the head (cornrows) were a symbolic representation of the land and indicated civilization. Cornrowing is an ancient art handed down from generation to generation. It is supposed to be a communication with the universe. Millions of women from West, South, East and Central Africa have braided their hair in cornrows for centuries (and still do).

In Mende Liberia, women liken their hair to vegetation. A beautiful head of hair is one that is thick, lush, and abundant, like the rice in a well-tended field. It is believed that a woman's coiffure encodes a prayer for abundant life and is thought of as demonstration for "the life force, the multiplying power of profusion, prosperity, and a 'green thumb' for raising bountiful farms and many healthy children. Thus, a woman's thick long tresses symbolize fertility and strength.[4]

Nigeria for example, looks upon this hairstyle as an art akin to spirituality and ritual. Traditionally among the Yoruba people, priestesses and queens wore the most numerous, elaborate and intricate cornrow styles.[5]

According to Camille Yarbrough, in her book, *Cornrows*, she states that in Ancient Africa it was believed that spirits took on many forms. Some of their symbols took on the forms of carved idols, sculpture ware, ritual masks, and in braided hair. You could tell the clan, the village just by the style of hair they wore. You would know if the woman were the queen, a princess, or a bride. You would know the gods they worshiped by the pattern that they made in their hair.[6]

Because it is difficult for the African to do his or her own hair, hairdressing became a social order. One concern of this societal structure is that someone who is trusted handles his or her hair. They believe, in the wrong hands, hair may be used as a powerful substance to afflict its owner. A victim's hair is often included in charms or "medicines" of witchcraft. Witches are also said to rob graves to collect human parts, including nails and hair, to activate evil spirits, supernaturally create (spirits) to act on their behalf. Thus, the "power" of hair is equated with the power of (a) life.[7]

In the Usambara Mountains of northeastern Tanzania, Shambaa healers are empowered by spirits. When a demon possessed healer, in this case, a woman, conjures up the spirits to perform a healing, she unties her head wrap to release long strand of braids, some artificial, that tumble out around her head and shoulders.

It's interesting that Shambaa women mostly wear their hair cropped and covered in a cotton head wrap. But when a demon possessed lady does her healing she wears her hair in the style that the spirit demands. She states if she doesn't do the things it wishes, "then I will get sick…and he will not help me in healing my patients."[8]

In my book, *My Hair, My Glory*, I state that witches don't cut their hair so that they can have power that is promised to women of God. The try to tap into this very power. I even discovered that in their witchcraft books they quote the very scripture we hold dear in 1 Corinthians 11. They believe that the power on their head is doubled if it is shaken in the wind. I quote over 30 different sources i.e. New Age, Occult, Hindus, etc., which believe in the power on the head. (*For a complete study of the relationship of a woman's hair, power, and occult read **My Hair, My Glory***).

Because many women have asked me if we may or may not braid our hair, I thought it be good to see what the scholars declare. Let's journey into what the commentaries say about braiding hair in the following scriptures:

> ***"In like manner also, that women adorn themselves in modest apparel, with shamefacedness and sobriety; not with broide hair*** [Greek. A plait of hair; to twine or braid]***, or gold, or pearls, or costly array;"*** *(1Timothy 2:9).*

Next study verse,

> ***"Whose adorning let it not be that outward adorning of plaiting the hair*** [to twine or braid; elaborate braiding of the hair] ***and of wearing of gold, or of putting on of apparel;"*** *(1Peter 3:3).*

These scriptures are a little problematic because we just read where an entire continent, Africa, braids her hair. According to these scriptures, should the holy women of Africa stop braiding their hair? If not, what could the two apostles be talking about?

Here is what I've found. According to the *International Standard Bible Encyclopedia,* "it is clearly from Egyptian literature and monuments, and well as from the writings of Greek authors (esp. Herodotus), that the dwellers on the Nile had their heads shaved, and women wore wigs." It is believed that the "seven locks of Samson's head" were plaits of hair, which are still worn by young Bedouin warriors of the desert.[9]

Assyrians on the other hand, wore their hair very long, however when studying the monuments it is supposed that their people wore some false hair, a sort of headdress to add to the effect of the natural hair. [10] In Greek society, says the *New Unger's Bible Dictionary,* if an Athenian citizen did not wear his hair short, he would have been mistaken as a slave. The Greek women wore their hair in an extraordinary variety of fashions. Both Greek and Roman ladies tried to dye their natural dark hair to blonde by artificial means.[11]

The *Wycliffe Bible Commentary* says that the Hebrew

women always wore their hair long. They regarded thick, abundant hair as an ornament. It is supposed that the fashionable Hebrew women imitated their Roman neighbors by elaborately braiding their hair and curling artificial locks.[12] *Wycliffe* states that the true confession of godliness is not attending to ostentatious [boastful or splashy] dress and hair but rather attending to good works.

So what was the Apostles Paul and Peter saying in these two verses? The "outward adorning" should not be the main thing the Christian woman cares about. *Barnes Notes* declares that she should not have her heart set on dressing the outward [wo]man. Yet, the apostles also do not infer that she should neglect her personal appearance either. Religion [the Holy Ghost] in our lives promotes neatness, cleanliness, and a proper attention to our external appearance according to our circumstances in life as well as the internal virtue of the soul.[13]

Women of the East paid great attention to their hair, sometimes up to three days of work. Their hair was often plaited with great care, and arranged in forms decorated with spangles or with silver wire or tissue interwoven. *Barnes* states that Christian females are not to imitate those of the world especially in their careful attention to the ornaments of the head, which worldly females wear.

Perhaps wearing a mere single braid is not improper and can be a simple convenient way of wearing the hair. But it is the excessive care, which prevailed during Paul's day that he was teaching against. The women of his day set their heart on doing up their hair with ornaments, like gold, silver, pearls, beads etc. Hence, it may not be easy to set an exact limit of time to dressing hair but it is the way in which it is fixed. So this is perhaps why the two apostles censured outlandish styles and admonished godly living.

Barnes' final comment on the subject is a good one. He said those whose hearts are right [before God] generally, have little difficulty on the subject. In other words, when the heart is right you want to dress in a way that is pleasing to Jesus and not flashy so that the whole world looks at you. *Hey, it's not about you anyway but about JESUS!*

Adam Clarke's Commentary noted that plaiting of the hair was an ancient practice that every part of the east was involved in, and so it is in present-day India, China, and also Barbary (a region of northern Africa on the Mediterranean coast between Egypt). Many plates, scholars have found, show the different modes of dressing the hair. Many however, were similar among the Egyptians, Greeks, Romans, Persians, and other nations. Thin plates of gold, believed to be the skin of the gods,[14] were often mixed with the hair, to make it appear more ornamental by the reflection of light and of the solar rays. Small golden buckles were also used in different parts; and among the Roman ladies, pearls and precious stones of different colors.[15]

The *Pulpit Commentary* states the ladies of that time seem often to have had their hair dressed in a very fantastic and extravagant manner. Although the mass of believers at this time belonged to the poorer class, there must have been a proportion of persons of rank and wealth among the Christians of Asia Minor. So the apostle asserts the utter worthlessness of hair embellishments as compared with Christian virtue and graces.[16]

Jamieson, Fausset, and Brown Commentary say she should not have the showy and costly apparel but have the blush of modesty instead of paint, and moral worth and discretion instead of gold and emeralds. Moreover, they declare sternly, such gaudiness characterizes the spiritual harlot (Rev 17:4).[17]

We know that having a love for the world does not please our Lord. In fact the Bible says, ***"Love not the world, neither the things that are in the world. If any man love the world, the love***

of the Father is not in him" (1 John 2:15). Here is how the Amplified Bible says it, *"Do not love or cherish the world or the things that are in the world. If any one loves the world, love for the Father is not in him."*

Because love is a verb, our actions demonstrate whom we love and whom we will serve.

> Again the book of Romans chapter eight reminds us, ***"For they that are after the flesh do mind the things of the flesh; but they that are after the Spirit the things of the Spirit. For to be carnally minded is death; but to be spiritually minded is life and peace. Because the carnal mind is enmity against God: for it is not subject to the law of God, neither indeed can be. So then they that are in the flesh cannot please God."*** (Romans 8:5-8).
>
> The Amplified version states it a little more clearly, *"For those who are according to the flesh and controlled by its unholy desires, set their minds on and pursue those things which gratify the flesh. But those who are according to the Spirit and [controlled by the desires] of the Spirit, set their minds on and seek those things which gratify the (Holy) Spirit. Now the mind of the flesh [which is sense and reason without the Holy Spirit] is death—death that comprises all the miseries arising from sin, both here and hereafter. But the mind of the (Holy) Spirit is life and soul-peace [both now and forever]. [That is] because the mind of the flesh—with its carnal thoughts and purposes—is hostile to God; for it does not submit itself to God's Law, indeed it cannot. So then those who are living the life of the flesh—catering to the appetites and impulses of their carnal nature—cannot please or satisfy God, or be acceptable to Him" (Romans 8:5-8 Amplified Bible).*

So according to these scriptures there is the dividing line. No one can sit on the fence. If a woman's heart is right before

God she would not go after the things of this world. She wouldn't want to be like, look like, imitate, or associate with the world and its ideas. That includes hairstyles, fashions and the like. This is not a black or white, Afrocentric or Eurocentric, issue but a Heavencentric issue. There is a line being drawn in the sand that is dividing the saved and the unsaved. According to the aforementioned scriptures these actions will not please God. It's up to each of us to seek after God, see what He requires and then, choose which side you're going to be on.

We are going to move into the most sensitive part of ***Her Ebony Glory***, partly because it's where we live. We, as women of God, want to look holy, godly in this present world. We want to shine our lights. And what woman does not want to look ***like*** a woman? And what woman doesn't want to act like a woman? The sensitive part is knowing that the one trait of a woman is her *hair*. And I'm saying this in love.

Tell me, what woman out there wouldn't want womanly hair? That is a redundant question. I know I did. *Read my testimony in my other book,* **Daring Dos.** My hair looked like chicken feathers. AND IT NEVER GREW! The kids (and neighborhood parents) used to call me "chicken" all the time. Not because I was a coward, but because of what my hair looked like! Hey, that scarred me, big time! I couldn't help it. My hair just didn't grow. And when it did, it looked like I brushed it with an eggbeater.

When someone says they just want long hair I know the feeling. I understand the women of the world, of course, may snub their noses at everyone, including God, and say it doesn't matter. They may say we can be, do, or look like *whatever* we what. That's true. God gives us free choice. But we must choose rightly. We must believe that it does matter. Those of us, who are endeavoring to live a clean, holy, upright life for Jesus, just want to do what is pleasing to Him.

It may be that in some cases a Jezebel spirit has crept into some churches. A black evangelist brother said to me that he (along with other preachers) fear to even dare to preach about black hair. But my reply to church ladies is, ***"...How shall they hear without a preacher?"*** (Rom. 10:14). How you gonna know if you won't let them teach. Someone must answer what nobody wants to ask. Hair is the touchstone of our lives. Let's not live in rebellion. Hearing brings faith, and faith brings deliverance and freedom.

Back to the issue at hand. Jesus wants us to look like his godly women. And our hair is the fundamental dividing point between looking like the world or looking like Apostolic women of God. We should allow our hair to look as close to what God created it to be at our birth. You may say, "girl, you mean you want my hair in a natural?" "Yikes!" Calm down, I promise you, we'll get to that subject. You might say, "Ok, but mine don't grow." I know, I heard that one hundred times. Or, "I want long hair and I will do whatever it takes to make it long." I realize that also. And I understand. Jesus understands.

Extensions and Weaves

Let's take a second look at the add-ons: braids, extensions, weaves and wigs. We already discussed the origin of wigs and braids. As far as I could find, the history of extensions (and weaves) is fairly new. In a way, it's a new modern phenomenon. I pinned it down to one lady in New York City.

According to an article, "Extensions," found in *New Yorker Magazine*, October 1991 stated that a lady named Barbara Terry of Harlem is claimed to have invented the extension braid. It is said that she also invented the Afro in 1961 when she was in too much of a hurry for a date to be bothered with her hair.

She ran out of the house with no time to hot-press her hair so she let it dry naturally and fluffed it out, and then as days passed, she just preferred wearing it that way. Consequently, people, she says would stop their cars and curse her out for wearing her hair in an Afro. The style caught on.[18] She later twisted her wet hair, and wore it like that. She says she got cursed out for wearing it like that too! Now, they call it "dreads."

Approximately thirty years later, she claimed, one day she dreamt she was walking down Seventh Avenue in Harlem and saw dozens of women parading down the streets all dressed up but the back of their head was missing. A voice said to her that she needed to do their hair.

She plainly asked how she was going to do that. And the voice said, "you need to braid it." When she woke from the dream, she went over to her mother's house, cut up an old wig and braided the wig hairs into her sister's short hair. It was styled into eight braids. She realized that she had just invented extension hair braiding—the use of synthetic fibers to extend short broken-off, over-processed hair. This made the hair more manageable. And as quick as a twist, the style caught on. And became an accepted Afro-American fashion.

Since then Ms. Terry developed her system, *Songa*

Original Undetectable Extensions Hair Braiding Technique. Extension braiding she states gives it [hair] length and structure and lets you do anything with it. It takes hours to get braided, but the braids last six or eight weeks, through dozens of shampoos. Finally, Ms. Terry retorts, "black people ruined their hair pressing and perming it, all because they were trying to look like Donna Reed. That's over. Extension braiding is the biggest thing since bubble gum!"[19]

That was a quick snap shot of the history of extension braids. Weaves were simply unknotted braids woven into the hair to add length. This was first invented to be a quick fix on women suffering with female pattern of baldness or other hair thinning problems. Their hair was not able to carry the thick braids, so the loosen braid strands of hair were woven or sewn into the hair itself. Weaves also omitted the use of heavy synthetic wigs.

So with that, is it wrong to want long hair? No. Is it wrong to wear false hair? Well, only if it doesn't hurt your only glory. Is there such a thing as false/fake glory? What does God think of false glory? Doesn't the fake hair cause damage to the real hair? Does this sound like a contradiction?

According to my friend, Colonel Tywana Bowman, "this common hairstyle amongst the ebony race, that is, chemically treated hair and application of wig extenders, will eventually cause breakage."[20] Andre Walker, Oprah's hairdresser, says, "I hear people say, 'You should see my hair underneath this weave, it's really grown.'" "If it's really grown." Andre states, "why not take off the weave? Let down your hair for awhile. You've got to come out from under your weave at some point. Why would you want to pretend it's your own hair?"[21]

The desire to have instant long hair in this 21st Century has made many hair companies millionaires. The surging weave business declares, *"if you can't grow it, fake it."* That is the way many women feel, saved or unsaved. The only way to have long hair is to get it woven in. However that is not what Barry Fletcher, an award-winning stylist and educator says. He declares, *"Don't sew it—grow it!"*

We will discuss how to grow your own hair in the next few chapters. There are many black hair care books that are promoting growing 6" of hair in one year. We will find out that this is not just a lot of hype but **truth**.

Before we learn how to grow out our own hair, Sister Betty Crawford of Providence, Rhode Island is going to share her testimony of what happen after she got saved. **"Coming Out of the Wig"** tells us about how the Lord helped her come out and grow her hair back. She will help those sisters of color who want so desperately to *"come out of the wig."*

---

[1] Rodrick Owen, Roderick Owen, Braids: 250 Patterns from Japan, Peru & Beyond, (Interweave Press, November 1995)
[2] www.telusplanet.net/public Indian History.
[3] James M. Freeman, *Manners and Customs of the Bible*, (Logos International: Plainfield, NJ, 1972) p254.
[4] *Hair in African Art and Culture*, eds Roy Sieber and Frank Herreman (Museum for African Art, New York, 2000) p72.
[5] Valerie Thomas-Osborne and Carla Brown, *Accent African Traditional and Contemporary Hairstyles for the Black Woman*, (Cultural Expressions, Inc. New York, 1992) p5.
[6] Camille Yarbrough, *Cornrows,* (Coward, McCann & Geoghegan, Inc. New York, 1997)
[7] *Hair in African Art and Culture*, eds Roy Sieber and Frank Herreman (Museum for African Art, New York, 2000) p139.
[8] Ibid, p147-148.
[9] "Hair," *International Standard Bible Encyclopedia, 1996.*
[10] Ibid.

[11] "Hair," *New Unger's Bible Dictionary*, 1988.
[12] "Hair," *Wycliffe Bible Commentary,* 1962.
[13] *Barnes Notes*, Electronic Database, 1997.
[14] Linda Reed, *Pagan Women*, CD-ROM.
[15] *Adam Clarke's Commentary*, Electronic Database, 1996.
[16] *Pulpit Commentary,* Electronic Database, 2001.
[17] *Jamieson, Fausset, and Brown Commentary,* Electronic Database, 1988.
[18] "Extensions," *New Yorker Magazine,* October 1991, p32-33.
[19] Ibid.
[20] Ebony Hair, Col. Tywana Bowman, e-mail October 5, 2002.
[21] Andre Walker, *Andre Talks Hair,* (New York: Simon & Schuster, 1997) p148.

More Answers

Sometimes you've got to let everything go—purge yourself... If you are unhappy with anything...whatever is bringing you down, get rid of it.

Because you'll find that when you're free, your true creativity, your true self comes out.

—Tina Turner (1939-)
Quotes from Famous Black Americans

Chapter 14

Coming Out of the Wig

(A testimony by Betty Crawford and retold by Juli Jasinski)

I believe God wants our glory, our hair to be in the best shape it can be, regardless of the color of our skin. Skin is not our glory but hair is our glory. Therefore, He is no respecter of persons. He has done it for others and He will do it for you. People are destroyed for lack of knowledge. And that means lack of any knowledge. I believe that if we apply the information Juli has written in this book, we will see a change in our hair and that change is about to explode throughout the whole body of Christ. Something big is about to happen! I am writing this from experience. I know what I am talking about; I am an eyewitness to it.

Coming out of the wig is a drastic move for some Apostolic African American women. Due to my profession before I was saved I always basically wore wigs. I was a singer in a band that was on the road traveling a lot. So wigs for me were a mere convenience, and yet at the same time, I sadly often neglected taking care of my own glory!

Making the initial decision to come out of the wig was a fearful thing. I wondered what people were going to think. If they saw me with my short hair in its real (damaged) state, would they think less of me? The devil plagued my mind with bad thoughts. I didn't even want to go to church for awhile. But the Lord reassured me that it would be all right. Sisters don't let the devil beat you with a hammer about what people are going to think. He is a liar. People are normally kind and understanding. It's ok to be transparent with God's children. They'll understand and probably pray along with you about it. Just be obedient to God and he'll take care of the rest.

Another reason I struggled from coming out of the wig was probably because I had one wig in particular that I loved. It looked so natural. When I wore it, people thought it was my hair. And although it was not human hair but made of synthetic fiber, this one was my favorite. To me, my wigs always looked good. I took care of them.

I soon realized that my wigs were damaging my hair. When one puts a wig or any synthetic fiber up against human hair it dries it out then causes it to break off. The constant rubbing of the wig's netting against the scalp also causes a receding hairline. So breaking hair and receding hairline really makes a person stay under cover. And in some cases, stay in the bondage of shame and embarrassment. But God wants for us to be brave and do what it takes to get your own hair growing. He will help us to get it to be glorious, and be that way for **His glory!**

Coming out of the wig is really quite simple. Here is what I did. First, I *wanted* to come out of the wig. God gave me the desire. I had to overcome fear and depend of God's strength to help me through. I remember some helpful hints my ex-hairdresser Jean told me. By following her advice, she helped me grow some hair.

My hair grew and became so nice. It even looked like a wig. It was fuller, thicker and longer at the end of one year. I saw results as each month passed. I was so excited I wanted to wear it out a few in between times so that everybody could see it growing.

During the time I spent in Thailand singing in my band, I did not take care of my hair like I had before in the United States. I did not have a good hairdresser overseas. It's important to have a hairdresser that knows what they are doing and knows how to deal with our hair type. I did get it done in a Thailand Salon, but they really did not know how to handle black hair.

Later, I found a lady who could add extensions. She was real good, so after a while I would just keep the braids in. But I kept noticing that my hair was not as well maintained as when I was in America. I didn't have the proper products or informed help that I needed for my hair type. That's when I resolved to just wearing the wigs. But soon, God dealt with me about them also.

When I came back from Thailand after being filled with the Holy Ghost and being baptized in Jesus name, I wore my hair in braids. Months later I noticed my hair was so dry. That's when I realized, to a degree, braids also can damage hair and cause breakage. *(So perhaps the Lord is not dealing with you about wigs, but about wearing extensions. This technique can also be applied to coming out of braids).*

In order to get my hair growing, this is what I did. (Thanks to Jean.) If you are going to wear a wig, while you're trying to grow your own hair out, there is a way to get your hair growing. First, wash and deep condition your hair. Have your hairdresser braid your hair in a circle, starting behind the ear and rotating until the circle reaches the crown of the head. Plan to keep (wear) it that way for months. Gently wash and condition your hair during each week, if possible let air dry every third day. Washing and conditioning your circle-braided hair helps it to grow.

After a month, let the hairdresser take out the braids, wash your hair again, condition it and braid it back up again. Keep your hair that way for 3-6 months, or even one year. You'll see a difference. The hair is protected as well as cared for by proper conditioning. You should see at least up to 6" of new hair growth in a year!

While you are growing out your hair long enough so that you can do something with it, it's good to put something between your hair and the wig. The important tip that I found out from my hairdresser is to line the rim of the wig with satin. And cover your natural hair (after you have had it shampooed and conditioned well) with a skullcap and then the wig. This will protect your hair from rubbing against the wig's netting which is so harmful. It dries out your hair—then the hair breaks off!

I found that you can buy two skullcaps or conditioning caps for .88 cents at *Wal-Mart* or at the *Family Dollar* for as cheap as two for a dollar. Before the days of skullcaps, I learned that you could cut the legs out of an old pair of panty hose and sew up the hole or tie it in a knot. The hair will now be protected. For double protection, wear a skullcap to bed and sleep on a silk pillowcase.

Another important reason you want to wear a skullcap is because it will prevent your hair from balding at the temples. This is very common since the friction from the wig rubs against the hair. The hair is rubbed off and causes scar tissue. The result…no hair grows back.

I learned all this from my former hairdresser, who has since retired. But thank the Lord for what I've learned from her. A lot is confirmed in all of the books Juli Jasinski recommends. I understand each person is different and may not affirm all that is said. But the bottom line is that hair is hair. And hair is what you want to grow. More than that, IT'S YOUR GLORY! And it needs to be taken care of properly. Find out what works for you and stick with it! The Lord is going to bless your glory, you will see!

The TIME IS NOW! We must stop interrupting the growth of our hair by abusive practices. When hair breaks off, outwardly it is shortened and then we have to start all over again. When hair is dry and brittle, it breaks and therefore, hinders the growth process. And we learned that the scripture teaches that the woman should have hair that is uninterrupted from growing. We want to get to the point where our hair just continues to grow on and on and on without any interruption at all.

I'm reminded of a sister that has beautiful long, thick, luxurious blonde hair. She has no split ends whatsoever. Her hair feels like silk. I asked her what she does to her hair. I'll never forget her words. She simply replied, "Sister Betty, I always take care of my hair." She spends the special time it takes with her hair and she is careful handling it.

She told me she uses the good products too. I asked her what she uses. I immediately said "I couldn't use that … black hair is different than your hair." She said, "it's really good, just try it." So I did try what she gave me.

It made a believer out of me. It's called *3-Minute Miracle* conditioner by *Aussie* (you can buy it at Wal-Mart). I used it. That product made a world of difference in the way my hair feels and looks (and it smells great). I later bought the whole line of products. The shampoo, conditioner, leave-in conditioner and detangler too. I didn't think it would work on black hair. And I have to say it really works on our hair. My hair came out soft, shiny and easy to comb.

And for an added bonus testimony, Sister Juli had a new convert sister come to her house for me to help her with her hair. Ann was made a believer that night. She said that in her country of Kenya, they only washed their hair with hand soap. *That stuff wrecks havoc on your hair.* So unbeknownst to her, that's what she used on her hair here in America up 'til now. She said she could NEVER put a comb through it. She became very frustrated.

We both (Juli and I) tried to comb out her hair before we washed it. It was thick as a rug. We couldn't finger rake *(run our fingers through)* her hair. We went to Wal-Mart bought the complete set of *Aussie* hair products. We washed, and deep conditioned her hair. Praise the Lord! We could actually comb her hair out with one conditioning.

That stuff is truly a miracle. I later straighten her hair and Juli fixed her hair in a few common Pentecostal hairdos. It brought dear Sister Ann to tears. She never believed that she could do that with her 4 1/2" hair. *(See pictures).*

Hey, you know what? You can do that too. So get growing your hair. You could get six inches in a year. By the year 2006 you could have a foot of hair. You could do all kinds of fun up-dos. Just be patient and grow some hair, girl!

This book is a blessing. We must take heed to how we handle His glory! It's not just hair. The Bible says that our hair is our glory. For where the glory of the Lord is, the Cherubims are there also. And they are protectors of God's glory and holiness (Psalms 99:1). He also tells us that we are to be holy for He is holy. And because of this we have power on our head! The angles stand in awe gazing down at us.

This information has come to us, Apostolic African American women for **such a time as this**. This world is about to be ushered into a revival like never before. And the sisters of all colors are going to play a major part in what the Lord is doing in our midst. God is getting ready to turn this world upside down with His Gospel.

We've got to unite. The spirit of unity is very important. When one member of the body suffers, the whole body suffers. If all the sisters are doing what we're supposed to be doing with our hair (protecting our glory) then there should be no room for shame, fear, and yes, even jealousy.

When I first got out of the wig and braids, the devil was on me like white on rice. "Look at you now" he said, "everybody's going to look at your hair." All the time he was lying. People aren't "looking" at my hair. He knows it is a sensitive subject with us. I hope Jesus is looking at us!

Yes, I myself admit I like long hair. I've always liked hair. When I was younger I once had long hair down my back. I would like it to be that length again. I just want healthy, long and luxurious hair that will bring glory to God.

Remember long hair is UNCUT, UNSTOPPED, and UNINTERRUPTED! Long hair comes as a result of hair that stops breaking off. Therefore if you want hair down your back then you can have it. You just need to take care of it properly so it won't break off.

There is another important factor I must add that shouldn't be forgotten in obtaining this goal. It is nutrition. Our diet is just as important, the Lord showed me that. And I hope someday to write a book about that very thing.

Thank the Lord for my retired hairdresser. I learned so much from her. I can see now how that knowledge, along with what Sister Juli has brought to us, is definitely for this time. To God Be the Glory.

Finally, tradition is another thing that stops us from growing hair. We'll say my grandmother did it this way, or my mother did it that way. The way they did their hair was a past custom. Forget about the way things used to be. Those practices have been proven to be harmful to your hair. Our point is to grow hair not to make it break off.

You are a new creature in Christ old things are passed away and behold all things have become new. You must learn to **STOP TAMPERING WITH YOUR GLORY.** He wants to work on your behalf, therefore let Him work.

What a testimony this can be for the women of color in the world! They will see us with long hair and be amazed. Then you can tell them what the Lord has done for you, not just with your hair but in your life. It's a great opportunity to witness!

So for those of you who wear wigs, braids, extensions or weaves, you can get your hair to grow and be very luxurious. It's going to take some time and much effort on your part, but **In Jesus Name, YOU can do it and it will grow.** And more than anything it will be healthy and bring glory to your Heavenly Father. Follow these simple steps:

1. **Pray and Ask the Lord to give you wisdom, understanding, knowledge and the right attitude toward this drastic change.**
2. **Get the right products for your hair, no matter the expense and follow the directions.**
3. **Choose how you are going to wear your hair.**
4. **Read all the books Juli Jasinski recommends.**
5. **Change your diet to a healthier one.**
6. **Be Consistent. Don't Stop Trying to Grow Hair.**
7. **Be Patient (practice patience while your hair is growing)**
8. **Do not let fear, shame or what others say bother you.**
9. **Thank the Lord in advance and Trust Him for your long, healthy head of hair.**
10. **Bless your hair in Jesus Name everyday—Don't curse it!**

I bless you in Jesus name!
Betty Crawford
Providence, RI

I used to want the words "She tried" on my tombstone. Now I want "She did it."

—Katherine Dunham (1910-)
Quotes from Famous Black Americans

Chapter 15

Making the Change

By simply making a few changes we believe that any black sister can have long hair. First, there must be an understanding of some facts about hair itself. With this knowledge, once applied, she will be able to see for herself the results. It will bring a dramatic change in her life.

Many of the black hair care books that I've read which promote hair growth first try to dispel some old thoughts about hair. In order for there to be any kind of change there must be a change of thinking. This is called a **paradigm shift.** One must cross over the bridge from thinking one way to thinking another. You cross over from an old way of doing something to a new way of doing it.

We are not unfamiliar with this concept. For example, Jesus said in order to get to heaven we must be born again. This is going from doing things one way (living the sinner's life) to living for Jesus. Being born again is following the simple plan laid out in Acts 2:38. When we make this change in our life we can call it a paradigm shift.

I want to share with you what the word "paradigm" means. According to Joel Barker, in his book, *Paradigms—The Business of Discovering the Future*, he states,

> *A paradigm is a set of rules and regulations (written or unwritten) that does two things: 1) It*

establishes or defines boundaries; and 2) it tells you how to behave inside the boundaries in order to be successful. A paradigm shift, then, is a change to a new game, a new set of rules. If you see a person messing with the rules, watch out, because that is the earliest sign of a significant change.

And, when the rules change, the whole world can change. And sooner or later, every paradigm begins to develop a very special set of problems that everyone in the field wants to be able to solve and no one has a clue as to how to do it.

Every paradigm, will, in the process of finding new problems, uncover problems it cannot solve. And those unsolvable problems provide the catalyst for triggering [another] paradigm shift.

New paradigms put everyone practicing the old paradigm at great risk. The higher one's position the greater the risk. The better you are at your paradigm the more you have invested in it, the more you have to lose by changing paradigms.

Those who choose to change their paradigms early do it not as an act of the head but as an act of the heart. To be a paradigm pioneer one allows the scales to fall from your eyes.[1]

Here is a classic example that Joel Barker gives in his book of paradigm shifts:

By 1968 Switzerland dominated the world in watchmaking for the past sixty years. The Swiss made the best watches in the world. Anyone, who wanted a good, accurate watch bought a Swiss watch. Remember the old wind up kind?

They constantly improved their watches with minute hands then second hands. Their watches had superior gears, bearings, and mainsprings. And the Swiss were on the cutting edge of waterproofing their watches also.

They had some 65 percent of the unit sales in the world watch market and more than 80 percent profit. They were the world leaders in watchmaking by an enormous stretch. No one came close to second them.

But in 1980 the bottom fell out.

They had a **paradigm shift**—a change in the fundamental rules of watchmaking. The mechanical mechanism was about to give way to electronics. A Swiss watchmaker came up with a new way of making a watch using electronic quartz crystal in Neuchâtel, Switzerland. Yet, when the man presented the paradigm shift of making watches differently to the Swiss manufacturers in 1967 it was rejected!

Consequently, Japan got a hold of the idea from the man at a watch making convention and liked the idea. They built on the new paradigm shift and between 1979 and 1981, perfected it. Seiko led the charge in the change and today, the Japanese have about 33 percent of the market, with an equivalent share of the profits. The Swiss, on the other hand, ended up laying off 52,000 workers! [2] Thus, began the era of digital time keeping and the old wind up watches…where are they today?

Get the picture? The Swiss refused to look at more than one way of making watches. The Japanese however, saw it differently, acted on it, and made millions of dollars.

<u>Here is some more paradigm one-liners by leaders recorded in Barker's book:</u>

"The phonograph...is not of any commercial value."
—Thomas Edison, 1880

"Flight by machines heavier than air is unpractical and insignificant."
—Simon Newcomb, 1902

"I think there is a world market for about five computers."
—Thomas Watson, chairman of IBM, 1943.

"Who the h--- wants to hear actors talk?"
—Harry Warner, Warner Brothers Pictures, 1927

"There is no reason for any individual to have a computer in their home."
—Ken Olsen, president of Digital Equipment Corp., 1977[3]

These men, no doubt experts in their field, couldn't see past their paradigms. We can readily apply this principle to black ladies hair care practices. Going back after slavery the black lady was free to roam. Her new life began and slowly emerged. She was learning "how to" be an American.

Madam C. J. Walker did her best in instilling dignity into the black women of her day. She very plainly felt the need for a change in order to solve the problem of losing her hair. It was not only her hair she discovered that had its troubles but other black ladies also.

She knew that black hair had a different texture and needed a different kind of handling to get it to looking its best. She found that by applying heat to her hair, and pressing it that would make it longer. Now she could handle it more easily and with a little more length, she could something with it. Thus, she invented the "hot-pressing comb."

However, she took a lot of flack from others by bringing about a paradigm shift. Everybody tried to say she is "trying to look" white. The male entrepreneurs said she couldn't have a company of her own, "she's a woman." And all the woman was just trying to do was grow some hair!

Being a true paradigm pioneer, Madam Walker stayed focused, perfected her hair care products and procedures, trained others, and went on to become the first black female millionaire. As we learned in chapter nine, her legacy was short lived, and her products died out, but the pressing comb lives on 'til this day.

Here is a little history of black hair in recent years. The "press and curl" style became the industry standard up into the 60's. For fifty years this new way of caring for African-American hair became a way of life. Ten years earlier before the "Afro" era, in 1950, another straightening process was invented. The Walker-hot-comb era was soon to be overshadowed by the discovery and development of chemicals known as "perms" or "relaxers." It was developed to help ease tight, curly hair.[4]

However, it wasn't until after the Afro era those chemical hair treatments caught on. The Afro era was an age of racial violence, Jim Crow laws and segregation that African-Americans suffered. No straightener could ease the revolution about to happen or stop the paradigm shifts this country would face. The United States was in an uproar during the 60's. Although Afros were a controversial style during this decade they soon caught on and became a fashion statement.

By 1977, Jheri Redding started the cold-wave curl along

with Willie Morrow creating the California curl. These styles were to maintain the curly texture of the Afro but simulate shiny, soft, glossy, tamed curls. The problem with this style was that a sticky, drippy moisturizing spray had to be applied daily along with an activator solution that kept the chemically straight hair curl. One had to wear plastic caps or bags on their head for long periods of time. Without the moisturizer the chemically treated hair would dry out and break off.[5]

Nowadays, with the end of apartheid, people wear their hair in a way that suits their taste and life style. We hear a lot about going back to **natural** hair care but this does not mean an Afro style. By this they mean, wearing your hair in its natural God-given chemical-free state. Don't hold your breath on this one, if God created it can't he help you care for it?

In the next chapter we'll find out how. Now let's cross over the bridge to a whole new way of caring for our hair.

---

[1] Joel Barker, *Paradigms—The Business of Discovering the Future,* (New York: Harper Collins Publishers, 1992) p32, 37-39, 51-52.
[2] Ibid., p15-17.
[3] Ibid., p89.
[4] Diane Carol Bailey, *Natural Hair Care and Braiding*, (New York: Milady Publishing, 1998) p7.
[5] Ibid., p9.

You're either part of the solution or part of the problem.

(Leroy) Eldridge Cleaver (1935-1998)
Quotes from Famous Black Americans

Chapter 16

Dispelling the Myths

Our dilemma as the church of the Living God, is not so much worrying how the world is doing their hair in the myriad of styles but what are we going to do about our hair. The point is how are we going to get our hair, our glory growing out without damaging it or drying it to the bone and causing it to break off. The solution, unfortunately, is not in a "quick-fix" answer. That mode of thinking is useless and usually ends up at a dead end road.

Most black ladies have been, for the most part, unsuccessful in getting their hair in the healthiest condition. Finding simple solutions has been not only a heavy burden but also a very costly one. Consequently, they've grabbed up the first remedy advertisement only to find it to be disguised in a smoky cloud of hype.

It's interesting to note, African-American women make up 15% of the American population and end up buying over 37% of all hair care products and the average Afro-American woman washes her hair only once every seven to ten days. Most hairstyles worn by women of color are very pricey to upkeep.

A lot of the trendy styles today are enhanced by, and advertised as, the pride of African ancestry. Therefore people are braiding, wrapping, twisting, weaving, locking, plaiting, and knotting their hair. This kind of pride leads one down the wrong path.

Here is what one woman, Akua-Adiki Anokye said in her book, *African Hairstyles*,

> *"We must resist all those forces which continue to oppress, suppress and repress us as an African people with a great, proud and significant past. We must resist assimilation and acculturation, as they have proven to be meaningless time and time again. We are what we are in the eyes of the oppressor. In our own eyes we should be what we are and reflect such. Then no one will come along and claim what belongs to us, be it art, culture, or land."*[1]

In order to grow hair, it's going to take time. First let's look at the myths that have been past down unchallenged throughout the generations. If you would allow a paradigm shift in your own thinking you will be able to find good hair care techniques and reach your goal.

In order to dispel the Myths we must first know what some of them are. Here is a dozen to start with:

1) **Trimming your [split or dead] ends helps your hair grow.**
**That's a lie, hair grows from the top not the bottom of your hair.*
2) **Black hair is different.**
**That's a lie, while black hair's texture is different, hair is hair.*
3) **Black hair doesn't grow.**
**That's a lie also, hair grows, red, yellow, black or white, all hair grows 1/2" per month under normal conditions.*
4) **I can't use a curling iron to hot press my hair.**
**That's a lie, keeping it on a low 150 degrees allows more temperature control than the old fashion stove method which has less control.*

Lisa Akbari mentions some myths too in her book *The Black Woman's Guide to Beautiful Hair.*[2]

5) **I was born with "bad" hair.**
**That's a lie, all hair is God-given, and is good.*
6) **Hair grows better when it's dirty.**
**That's a lie, hair grows better when kept clean.*
7) **Hair breaks because I have a nerve problem.**
**Lord have mercy, you know that ain't true, manage your stress and your hair will grow.*
8) **Grease will make my hair grow.**
**That's a lie, grease and oil clogs the hair follicles, and stops growth.*
9) **All shampoos are the same, it doesn't matter what I use.**
**That's a lie, cheap shampoos have as much chemicals as perms.*

Here are a few myths Pamela Farrell talks about in her book, *Let's Talk Hair.*[3]

10) **Let the stylist take care of my hair, they know what they are doing.**
**Girl, you know that can't be right, they are most of the reason your hair is a mess, you need to learn self-styling hair care tips.*
11) **I can't grow hair if I'm partly bald or have bald spots.**
** That's a lie, get rid of poor hair care habits that caused the bald spots and you can grow hair.*
12) **My hair is too ugly to wear it natural, chemical-free.**
**That's a lie, once you learn how to care for it, you will notice how soft it is and that it has a unique style of its own.*

No doubt there are more myths or grandma's tales that are floating around but one must dismiss them for what they are. These myths have been proven to have no validity in them and to be false. Here is how hair grows.

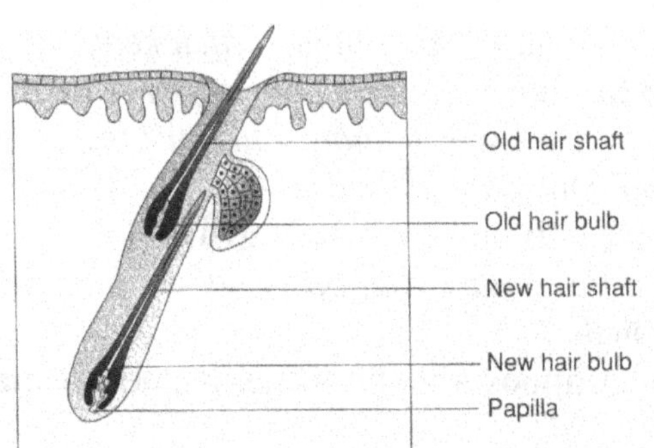

Growth cycle of the hair shaft—Picture 2

The factors that make up all hair types, whether the texture is straight, wavy, curly, or kinky, are the same and produced from little pockets in the skin called **follicles.** All **hair follicles** can be compared to a "factor" with the actual manufacturing part, the **papilla**, as its bulb-like base.

This dispels Myth #2 Black hair <u>is</u> the same as other hair types.

To think of the papilla as a 'root' is a misconception. Even when a hair is plucked out, the papilla stays behind and starts making a replacement hair. The papilla is rich in minute blood vessels.[4] Each hair follicle is supplied by one or more **sebaceous glands**, which produces the **natural oil** to lubricate the hair.

It is the oil produced by these glands that gives the hair its gloss and richness.[5] Brittle or dry hair often suffers from a

deficiency of sebum, whereas oily hair may result from an excess of it.[6]

A hair lengthens only because a new piece of shaft is continually emerging from the **papilla.** This, in healthy people, occurs at a rate of about **one half inch per month**, while in exceptionally fit people it can grow as much as seven or nine inches a year.

Myth #3 is tossed out 'da door, black hair grows!

The hair shaft consists of three layers; the outer layer, also called the **cuticle**, the second layer, called the **cortex**; and the innermost layer, the **medulla**. To each **follicle** is also attached a special muscle, the **arrector pili**. Hair muscles can be seen working very obviously and dramatically on cats and dogs, when fear or anger causes their fur to rise.

In humans it is more normally a response to cold that causes the muscles to contract, producing goose pimples and upstanding hair. But in moments of great stress the same effect may be achieved through the body's hormone response. Our hair can stand on end with fear. Stress can't stop the hair from growing but could make it stand at attention.

Myth #7, Don't even lie to me! Stress is no excuse for not growing hair.

Reports from World War II, for example, tell of memory-haunted men whose hair stood on end for several months after their experiences on the beaches of Dunkirk. A British army doctor, Sir Arthur Hurst, in his book Medical Diseases of War (1944), described similar cases from the trenches of World War I:

> *I saw several men suffering from the effects of severe emotional strain, whose hair permanently stood on end and could not be kept down by means of grease. In some cases I had the opportunity of comparing their appearance with what it was formerly, and the change from the sleek appearance when in civil life was most remarkable. One man, who kept his hair closely cropped, said his hair reminded him of the bristles of a hedgehog.... In some cases the hair of the body as well as the head has been persistently erect.*[7]

In the book of Job, he states, ***"Then a spirit passed before my face; the hair of my flesh stood up"*** (Job 4:15). When Job sensed a spirit nearby, he too, was frightened enough to make his hair stand straight up on end.

The **cuticle** is formed from tiny overlapping **scales**, similar to the scales of a fish or tiles on a roof.[8] If you have a microscope, find a hair that has fallen out in your brush, prepare a wet slide mount and place it under the microscope to view the scales on the cuticle. I couldn't help it I had to see it for myself. I discovered that there are scales on my hair!

If you want to feel the roughness of the outer layer, draw your fingers through the hair from end to scalp. It will give you a sensation of "going against the grain." Like fingernails, the **cuticle** is transparent, and does not affect the color of the hair.

When combed smooth, the hair looks soft and shiny but

when combed the wrong way, the hair can become dull and rough in texture. Improper handling of the hair and the use of harsh chemicals in hair dyes, perms, relaxers, and cheap shampoos can cause the layers of the cuticle to tear and loosen. When the hair is greasy, on the other hand, the cuticles tend to get clogged, giving a dull, lifeless appearance.[9]

It is in the **cortex**, the second layer of the hair shaft, that the hair's natural color matter, **melanin** is found. The cortex comprises a great many long fibers which give the hair strength and suppleness. The **fibers** of the cortex separate readily and appear to be held together by the **cuticle**. Buried within the numerous fibers is the **medulla**, the innermost layer composed of spongy, **cellular tissue**. Within the medulla there are very few **melanin-producing cells** to provide color. In very fine hair the medulla is often absent altogether.[10] (Perhaps no one knows this for sure but maybe the sun produces medulla. The hotter the sun the more medulla (color) one has. This could be why people groups who live near the equator have dark hair.

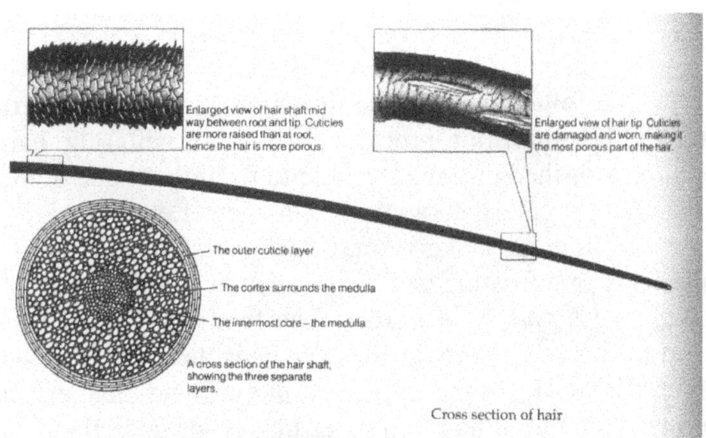

Cross-section of hair shaft—Picture 3

Here is the most interesting part of the study of the anatomy of hair. This information on follicles is very eye opening. The reason **perms** and **relaxers** don't work permanently is because you only temporarily change the shape of the **hair shaft** but not the **follicle** itself**.** You can't change the hair follicle. This is what everyone was born with. Isn't it interesting how God designed hair? Let's take a look at it.

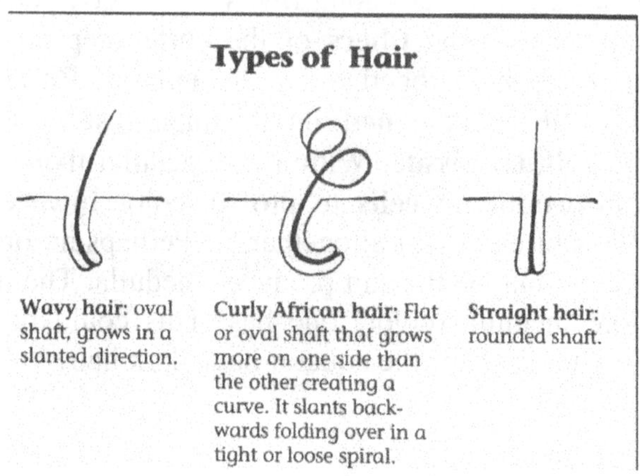

Types of Hair
Wavy hair: oval shaft, grows in a slanted direction.
Curly African hair: Flat or oval shaft that grows more on one side than the other creating a curve. It slants backwards folding over in a tight or loose spiral.
Straight hair: rounded shaft.

Types of hair—Picture 4

The <u>follicle</u> is the hole in which the hair grows out of. After the keratinization process (forming of cells) the hardened structure is pushed through the hole to form the shape of the hair. Remember the cake analogy I used in chapter eleven?

In order to make a pretty cake design; you must place white icing in a frosting bag, then use different decorating tips to squeeze out a variety of shapes. The frosting is pushed through the tip to form the desired pattern. This is the same idea with our **hair follicles**. It is the angle of the follicle that effects the configuration of the hair. No other black hair book that I've read addresses this physiological aspect of hair. This discovery bears repeating again.

If you were born with **stick straight** hair your follicle is **round**. If your hair is **slightly wavy** your follicle looks **less circle-like** and more like an oval. If you have **curly hair** your follicle is very oval looking.

And if your hair is **kinky** with tight **"s"** or **"z" curves** your follicles have openings that look like **slots** or **rectangles** making the hair shafts flat on the sides. The hair shaft curls into itself and not up and out straight.

This is why a ***perm will never permanently curl straight hair. Nor chemical straighteners or relaxers ever keep curly hair straight.*** It will inevitably ***grow out only to return to its natural God-given state***. Was this God's plan all along?

Unless you change the opening of the follicle, which is impossible, you'll always have hair that you inherited at birth. It was passed down through the DNA down your line of genetics. It will remain the same until you die.

No one has a magic formula to change the composition of your hair. It's only a temporary fix, which is VERY costly both monetarily and cosmetically. You need to be happy with what God gave you. What stylists have invented is a way to alter the shape only for a few months. As long as we are living hair will grow back to its natural state.

The growth cycle of hair is somewhat of a mysterious phenomenon that can better be described than explained. Every follicle on the head is independent of another. In other words, each of the 100,000+ hairs we have is mutually exclusive.

Each hair strand has a three-part growth-and-shed cycle. The process is continued until eventually the life of each **hair strand cycle** stops. If it wasn't for the simultaneous **growth-and-**

shed cycle occurring together then we'd all go bald periodically.[11]

Most hair specialists say that the hair-growth phases are staggered in a **mosaic pattern.** And thankfully so, because if the growth-and-shed cycle happened all at once, we would shed our hair and be bald from time to time. It would be a ghastly sight! I can see it now, if someone asked us if we were going to church on Sunday, we'd answer, *"No, I can't. I'm molting!"* Furry animals, on the hand, do go through a seasonal shedding of their winter coats.

The way the Lord created us ladies (and men) is that hair is growing continuously on our head at any given time. For men who go bald, experts say that the follicles don't die they just lie dormant. The current medical explanation for baldness is that accumulations of **androgenic hormones** in the bloodstream somehow permanently interrupt the continuity of the three-part growth-and-shed cycle.[12]

The first phase of the three-part cycle is called the **growth phase** or **anagen phase.** Rich in minute blood vessels, the papilla starts manufacturing amino acids that are synthesized into protein to feed the continuous formation of cells on the outer surface. These cells continuously being created from below push up the older ones, which, as they rise, undergo structural differentiation into the variously shaped cells that make up a hair shaft.

After a final hardening process, called "**keratinization**," the shaft emerges from the mouth of the follicle as a visible hair.[13] Just as your liver produces bile and your stomach produces digestive juices, so your follicles produce **keratin** that is the protein substance commonly called **<u>hair</u>**.[14]

If you deprive your bloodstream of **essential proteins** or calories due to an unbalanced and insufficient diet, your follicles won't produce good keratin.[15] This means that your hair is not nourished enough to keep it growing.

On the other hand those who **eat wisely** and **exercise**

regularly will cause their **blood to flow more rapidly and will produce richer keratin**, which **stimulates the hair to grow**. Grow, grow, and grow.

According to the Grolier Multimedia Encyclopedia CD-ROM, "Hair gets its color from a pigment called **melanin,** which is made by cells called **melanocytes** and is responsible for all the colors of hair from yellow to black. Hair turns gray when the **melanocytes** die."[16] *You'll learn more about gray hair later.*

The average rate of growth of a human hair for the duration of the **anagen phase** is only about a third of a millimeter per day. The length of each hair follicle's anagen phase varies significantly from one person to another, usually lasting somewhere between two and six years.[17] This is speaking of one strand of hair not the entire head of hair.

The next phase is the **transitional** or **catagen** phase. This cycle is brief perhaps lasting only a matter of weeks. During this period the catagen follicle winds down its rapid metabolism, wrinkles, contracts, and ceases the production of keratin. Catagen shrinkage is a natural part of the growth-and-shed cycle, which cannot be stopped.[18]

The final phase is called the **telogen** phase which occurs when the follicle stops shrinking. This is a period of rest and suspended animation in which the hair does not immediately fall out but rather sits in the now fully contracted follicle bulb. The typical length of the telogen phase is around three months, during which the hair will rest in the follicle until it's physically dislodged by brushing or washing.[19]

Normally we lose anywhere between 50 and 100 hairs from our head every day and the life span of any particular hair is unlikely to be more than six years and may be as little as two.[20] Be sure and know that every hair on your head is in one of these three-part growth-and-shed cycles.

This dispels Myth #3 Black hair grows the same as other types.

So now you ask why does Black hair break so much? Because black is beautiful yet exceptionally fragile and delicate. Every bend and coil of black hair is a weak link. Black hair under a microscope looks like the old fashion string of hot dogs. So think of your hair more like a chain link rather than a rope.

It will likely break before it's touched, let alone styled. That is why braiding, twisting, or pulling black hair is so bad for it. Hair straighteners can be severely damaging and over-processing is hair's death sentence. Black hair can hardly withstand a good brushing and barely survives a chemical treatment.

Contrary to a frequently held belief, neither shaving, trimming or cutting accelerates hair growth. How could cutting the bottom of the hair make the top of the hair grow? The hairs grow from the top of the head not the bottom of hair, therefore, it is a false assumption to believe a monthly trimming will cause the hair to grow faster.

Myth #1 (Oh, please) You can chuck that one out the window.

Even if hair was neither shaved, nor cut, nor plucked, a hair strand still has only a limited life span before it falls out naturally and is replaced by a new shaft [hair].[21] This information is helpful to dispel any anxiety particularly when we perceive gobs of our glory in the sink or at the bottom of the drain in the shower. Now we don't have to panic because we know it's a normal process of the growth-and-shed cycle.

Let's address the common complaint of women of color's hair: Why is it so dry? African hair is dry because the oily, waxy substance, **sebum**, from your oil follicles, does not make its way down the curly hair like straight or wavy hair. It should work its way down the hair shaft to lubricate the hair strand but the oil flow is hindered. The oil has to go around every coil, and every springy twist, making it nearly impossible. The oil never makes it.

So the hair feels dry, even when the scalp feels oily. Remember that the scalp and the hair are two different parts on your head. That is why greasing your hair, or using a hot oil treatment, are really a waste of time. Grease, sebum, dirt, pollution, stuff, and gunk can actually clog up the follicle opening, and cause the hair from being pushed out. The growth circulation is literally is choked off, and as a result, the natural hair growth can become stunted.

Myth #8, This one goes through the paper shredder. Grease does not cause hair to grow.

Over-processing the hair can hurt the scalp causing scar tissue, thus hindering new growth. Ever look at scars on your body? Hairs just don't seem to push through the skin—perhaps the follicles got ripped off. Chemically processed hair is especially delicate when wet hair. Because the hair bonds have been weaken in order to lay straight, the cuticle shingles are opened, and catch onto the roughened shingles of other hairs, and this is why the processed hair gets so tangled.

When African hair is chemically straightened, the dryness problem increases. The chemicals break down the keratin bonds in the cuticle so the curls will straighten out. The loss of keratin and the chemical process make your hair shaft dryer because the protective shingles are altered.[22]

Most of the shingles have been blasted open by the

chemical commandos making the hair shaft to lay straight. *This is a chemical warfare of another kind.* The natural sebum your body produces, is not enough for virgin chemical-free hair in its natural state. And it's near impossible, to correct the chemically induced dryness brought on by straighteners.

Since moisture is the opposite of dryness, that is what your hair needs. To say black hair lacks oil is a misconception. Dry hair needs moisture not oil. Think moisture, moisture, and more moisture. Once your hair has been chemically altered (i.e. relaxer, perm, or dyes) it can take up to one year to grow back a full head of natural hair. Some stylists believe that once your hair has been chemically treated there are no products, solutions, or procedures that will reverse the condition.

However, Sister Betty, our friend that we met in chapter 14, said that she heard someone say that washing your hair with vinegar can help clean the chemicals out. I have not found any books that teach how to remove the chemicals from the hair.

All of them say—just cut it off!!! **I don't believe we need to do that.** That is the world's solution. What you need to do is ask the Lord to give you wisdom on how to handle it. Eventually, the permed hair will break off and virgin hair will emerge.

Remember cutting off your glory causes bigger ramifications spiritually. That's not the answer. If you wait on the Lord he will help allow the chemicals to come out naturally. It's your choice. We want the angels nearby us to protect, to provide and to give us supernatural power. Don't we? Then don't cut it off.

Pamela Farrell says, "heat pressed or blow-dried hair is still considered natural. The hair retains its original texture and consistency. Braiding, twisting, and styling natural hair are healthy methods that physically change the hair appearance, but do not change the hair texture properties." The natural hair is styled nicely but left unharmed.[23]

Myth #11 is blown out of the water! Black hair is beautiful if it's taken care of.

Even if your hair is thinning, balding, or has been grossly abused by over-processing you still can grow hair.

Myth #10, don't you even think about hanging 'round here! Do all you can to promote hair growth on bald spots.

You can promote hair growth by first deciding to wash your hair every other day or every third day. Dirty hair tangles easy. Unwashed hair falls out frequently. But clean hair stays strong.

This dispels Myth #6 Black hair can be washed every other day or every third day.

Use an "everyday" spray conditioner—you'll see results.

Give yourself a scalp message. I've even tried a vibrating brush, but yikes, it rattled my teeth to death! This encourages blood circulation and stimulates the hair follicles. The result is growing hair. Grow, grow, grow.

Comb out (or soft brush) your hair everyday but not the proverbial 100 strokes. *White girls don't even believe that one anymore*. If you see too much little tiny hair on your shoulders your are brushing too, too hard. Cut back on the brushing, and just comb gently. Remember hair is not made out of steel girls, but think of it as silk. Spray hair with a moisturizer, this will keep it from drying out. Dried out hair breaks. Breakage keeps the hair short.

Exercise often, walk, swim, ride a bike or whatever. This promotes more blood circulation and the more blood pumping to the brain the more the hair will get nourished. When it's time to relax, lay with your feet up and head down. As a young girl, I remember being told lay on my bed and hold my head upside down for 5 minutes. That's not a myth but true. The blood flows to the scalp and hair follicles. This is great for your hair.

Please note that nutrition plays a very vital role in healthy hair. If your diet is poor your hair will suffer and will show it first. If your health is poor your body pulls its resources to fight the illness, and usually hair gets the proteins taken from it first. Joy Haney has an excellent book on health called *Radiant Health*. Read it and be healthy. Take your vitamins. Personally, I like taking herbs and drink a power shake twice a week for health.

If you got a bona fide nerve problem consult a physician. Stress is present in everybody's life these days. You need to learn how to manage stress. There are plenty of tapes, books and information on stress management at your local library. Once you relax, you'll realize your hair has been growing all along.

Myth # 7, Don't blame the nerves!

In respect for our beautiful graying sisters I have a special chapter for you. Read on.

[1] Akua-Adiki Anokye, *African Hairstyles.*
[2] Lisa Akbari, *The Black Woman's Guide to Beautiful Hair,* (Illinois: Sourcebooks, 2002) p64-66.
[3] Pamela Farrell, *Let's Talk Hair,* (Washington, D.C: Cornrows & Co. 1996) p106.
[4] Marion Matthews and Renske Mann, *Hair Magic,* (New York: Arco Publishing, Inc., 1984) p17.
[5] Wendy Cooper, *Hair: Sex, Society, Symbolism*, (New York: Stein and Day, 1971) p24.
[6] Matthews and Renske, p16.
[7] Cooper, p16.
[8] Matthews and Mann, p16.
[9] Ibid.
[10] Ibid.
[11] Jonathan Zizmor, M.D., and John Foreman, *Superhair: The Doctor's Book of Beautiful Hair* (New York: Berkley, 1978) p14.
[12] Ibid., p15.
[13] Cooper p23.
[14] Zizmor and Foreman, p13.
[15] Ibid, p14.
[16] "Human Hair Growth," *Grolier Multimedia Encyclopedia* CD-ROM.
[17] Zizmor and Foreman, p17.
[18] Ibid, p18.
[19] Ibid.
[20] Cooper, p 28.
[21] Ibid.
[22] Lonnice Bonner, Good Hair, p19.
[23] Pamela Farrell, Where Beauty Touches Me, (New York: Cornrows & Co., 1993) p17.

Picture Credits:

Picture 2—Diane Carol Bailey, Natural Hair Care and Braiding (Albany: Milady Publishing, 1998) p67.
Picture 3—Marion Matthews and Renske Mann, Hair Magic (New York: Arco Publishing, 1984) p17.
Picture 4—Lonnice Brittenum Bonner, Good Hair (New York: Three Rivers Press, 1991) p17.

Life is short, and it's up to you to make it sweet.

—Sadie Delany (1889-1999)

Quotes from Famous Black Americans

Chapter 17

For Graying Beauties

(Special Section)

What about all this gray? Do I dye it or not? Is gray hair double honor or double trouble? The Lord promises us that He'll carry us through when we are old. The book of Isaiah 46:4 states, ***"And even to your old age I am he; and even to hoar hairs will I carry you: I have made, and I will bear; even I will carry and will deliver you."*** Sooner or later, old age is accompanied with gray hair and comes to all of us.

Unfortunately, along with the gray hair, comes some perplexing questions for Pentecostal women: What are we going to do with the gray once it gets here? Are we going to gracefully accept it or go into denial and try to cover it up with hair dye? What does the Bible have to say about gray hair? If it is so glorious why do people dye it?

In the book of Proverbs 16:31 it states, ***"The hoary head is a crown of glory, if it be found in the way of righteousness."*** Many people have hoary or gray hair on their head but they are not walking in righteousness. So the sinner's crown is forfeited and it becomes a crown laid in the dust ... but if a person is found in righteous living, it's a glory to them. According to the Bible, white or gray hair is the symbol of honor and authority. And the wearer thereof is entitled to respect.

Gray hair is stated again in Proverbs 20:29, ***"The glory of young men is their strength: and the beauty of old men is the grey head."*** The Word of God says that gray hair is beautiful, and those who have it are ***"...worthy of double honour, especially they who labour in the word and doctrine"*** (1 Tim. 5:17).

I can remember being taught respect for my elders as a child. The eight years I went to parochial school, we would have to stand and greet the principle or teacher as they entered the classroom, chanting "Good Morning, Mother Gemma." Even if you go into a courtroom all the people present are required to stand in honor of the Judge entering the room. This shows respect for authority.

Perhaps the saying "Respect your elder" comes from the Old Testament•. This teaching is found in Leviticus 19:31, ***"Thou shalt rise up before the hoary head, and honour the face of the old man, and fear thy God."*** • This is a lesson to the young to show respect to the aged. The Jews were taught by God to treat the elderly with high regard. Those whom God has honored with the blessing of a long life ought to have honor shown back to them.

The godly• and the wise• are worthy of double honor. We are therefore obliged to adhere to good manners and respect for our elders, after all, that is what the Word of God teaches.

Clement of Alexandria stated in his letter, *The Instructor,*

> *And above all, old age, •which conciliates trust, is not to be•concealed. But God's mark of honor is to be shown in the light of day, to win the reverence of the young. For sometimes, when they have been behaving shamefully, the appearance of hoary hairs, arriving like an instructor, has changed them to sobriety, and paralyzed juvenile lust with the splendor of the sight.*[1]

For Graying Beauties

Gray hair is a normal sign of aging that typically shows up in the fourth decade of our lives. But a person can inherit a gene to cause them to go gray prematurely. There are also medical conditions that cause grayness. If you lack vitamin B-12 or vitamin D, you may have a yellow-complexion and your hair may be gray.

Another condition is thyroid disease, which causes premature grayness. Some experience excessive graying when they have been through traumatic events in their life. Though rare, there are cases of people "Going white overnight." These people experience this as a result of emotional trauma or physical shock and perhaps are in need of professional attention.[1]

Although the white hair is rich in phosphate sometimes the hair feels coarser than the hairs with color. It's usually because of increasing dryness from the natural decline of scalp oil secretions that accompanies aging. The dullness can be cured with adding some conditioner with moisturizers to replenish the natural oils.

What is gray hair? The gray hair is the process of decolorization in the production of hair. The color residing in the hair does not discolor. Even when hair is removed from the head, hair keeps its color for hundreds of years, so it is not correct to think that hair is fading.

Why does hair turn gray anyway? Graying occurs when the body slows down and eventually stops the production of color pigmentation in the hair follicle. It is the failure to deposit of the melanin (coloring agents) which form in the cortex (center) of the hair down in the base of the follicle and around the papilla.

Here is a thought. In the case of African, Asian, and Middle Eastern people still living in their countries, could it be that the hot sun keeps producing the melanin even in the older people? Could this why their elders seem not to gray until they reach 70, 80 years of age? (Just a thought.)

As we age, go through stressful times, lack the proper diet and vitamins, endure sickness or disease the hair cells become less and less active. The cells have everything essential to produce a hair. The cells send up out of the mouth of the follicle a hair which, in a sense, is only partly completed. The melanocytes (melanin producing cells) slow down and eventually die, thus sending up a hair that has no color in it.

The term "gray" is not really the proper term for hair. White describes it better because "white is the absence of color." Hence, white hair is absent of any hair coloring. We only call it gray because it looks this way against the other hues in our hair.

According to Dr. Leon Augustus Hausman, a professor of Zoology, Rutgers University, writes in his article "Why Hair turns Grey" which ran in the *Scientific American,* September 1925,

> *After the hair leaves its papilla ... above the surface of the skin, it is practically a dead structure. This is an important thing to remember. The hair's only connection with the body is that it is rooted in the scalp. It has no organic connection with the body. Neither nerves nor blood vessels run up into it. What is the significance? It means that no changes can go on in the hair after it leaves the surface of the skin ... thus, after it has grown out beyond the surface of the skin, the hair cannot change its color any more then the outer garments which you wear can change their color.*[3]

"Nobody knows why it [graying] happens," says Tony Ray and Angela Hynes in their book, *The Silver/Gray Beauty*

Book, "as of right now, there is no way to stop your hair from turning silver once your inherited time clock starts ticking."

I conclude that this is the Lord's way of letting us know that we've only got a few years on this planet earth to do His will. If we flounder through the decades, our gray hair is there to remind us that our time is short. Nothing is permanent. We need to get going and do something for God and not waste the years.

For many women, however, it's a time to hit the panic button when the gray hair makes its debut. Because the gray hits around forty years of age, many go through what the psychologists term "midlife crisis." But the scientists tell us that the aging process can't be stopped.

Along with gray hair comes the need for reading glasses, declining stamina, kids moving out of the nest, and we experience bodily aches and pains. There is nothing we can do about it. But many still panic, regress or go into depression. Or of course, run out to the beauty parlor and get the gray covered! But we ladies of a higher calling, children of the King, women of the One True God need not dread or fear, God is with us and we are worthy of double honor. Hey, I like that!

Now that we know about hair, dispelled pointless myths, learned how it grows, why it slows down, and why it turns gray, let's continue to learn how to care for our glory in the next chapter.

[1] Clement of Alexandra, *The Instructor*, vol. 2, p286.
[2] Zizmor and Foreman, p77.
[3] Leon Augustus Hausman, Ph. D., "Why Hair Turns Gray" *Scientific American*, September 1925, p307.

People pay for what they do,

and still more for what they have allowed themselves to become. And they pay for it very simply; by the lives they lead.

—James Baldwin (1924-1987)

Quotes from Famous Black Americans

Chapter 18

Caring for Your Glory

Because "lack of knowledge" has practically destroyed our hair we must be wise stewards and learn as much as we can to keep it healthy. We must be open-minded and teach ourselves the basics. Depending too much on hair stylists has been a big part of the problem. They are humans not gurus. I hate to say but many just love that "almighty dollar."

Oh yes, some of you may have had the best stylists at one time or another but what happened when he or she left town? Or retired? Or disappeared? What would happen if suddenly you were too broke to go to a salon? Or were like Sister Chase, whose husband was military and she moved around the world a million times and was at the mercy of every Tom, Dick or Harry to do her hair. Only to come home with balding sore spots across her head.

This is why I feel strongly that you must learn self-styling basics. Stop depending on the salon to do you some hair. This way you can actually become familiar with your hair type and free yourself from depending on someone else to always do your hair. Use a salon visit as a once in awhile treat, I do mean great while. Remember just because that's how they've always done it in the past, you don't gotta do it that way now. Break the cycle. Be a paradigm pioneer!

A popular myth to dispel, which is so ingrained in our mind is a dependency on a salon person to do something with your hair.

Myth # 10, Take a hike! I'm not a salon junkie I can do this!

Women who are not necessarily good at styling their own hair can learn at least one or more quick dos. At first, you'll feel like all thumbs but then you'll get used to it and enjoy the benefits. You will notice people's complements on your hair. Get a friend to help you. It's like a prayer partner, you can become hair partners.

What you'll need to grow hair:

Tools:

1) **Wide-tooth comb**. Wooden is best, reduces static but nylon is suitable.
2) **Natural boar bristle brush**. To be used sparingly, brushing too hard causes excessive breakage.
3) **Blow dryer** with diffuser attachment. To help loosen and smooth hair.
4) **Curling Iron.** With setting adjustment. To be used for straightening hair or curling ends.
5) **Butterfly clips**. For keeping hair sections separate.
6) **Bobby pins or hair pins**. For Up-dos.
7) **Elastic band for pony tails.**
8) **Hair clips or decorative combs.** For finishing touches.

Hair Care Techniques:

Shampoos are for cleaning the scalp while conditioners are for strengthening damaged hair and keeping healthy hair from becoming damaged. Don't go cheap. Buy the good ones. For the price of two or three boxes of kid's cereal you can buy some good shampoos. The cheap shampoos have as many chemicals as perms and relaxers do.

That is how they sell them so inexpensive. They use a fraction of the good stuff and mix it with additives and sell it for a cheap price. I never use that stuff. A good shampoo will have a 5.5ph balance. I buy my products from salons. There is a shampoo outlet at the mall in my town I like to go to. Wal-Mart also has a salon that carries good products.

Bye, bye Myth #9 Good shampoos do make a difference.

My hair grew over 18 inches after I wrote my second book, Daring Dos and discovered all these hair care tips—especially buying the good stuff! Good products means paying just a little more for quality.

If you're not sure what to buy ask the salon personnel. They are so helpful. Black hair needs moisture so buy the shampoos with moisturizers. Paul Mitchell, Back to Basics, Matrix, Aussie and many other name brands are good to try. Try them and see which one is best for your hair. Personally, I use them all. I like to switch shampoos every six weeks or less because of product build-up. The next shampoo will wash out the build-up and leave your hair nice and smooth. Using the same brand for an extended period of time will defeat its effectiveness.

A WORD OF CAUTION: Use the same shampoo and

conditioner together because the manufactures have formulated them to work together as a team. Ingredients in one brand may interact conversely with another brand. Use the same brands together. Don't mix and match.

Conditioners are great for adding moisture back into your hair and adding protein to the hair shaft. It is a great way to get hair healthy. Deep conditioners should be used from once a week to twice monthly depending on the hair's condition**. DO NOT OVER CONDITION YOUR HAIR.** If it says leave on for only three minutes, that's it, don't leave it on for any longer.

It will go limp and feel slimy. Always read the directions. You may use a heat-activated penetrating conditioner with a heating cap. Everyday conditioners are not as thick and should be used in weekly washings. On the days that you don't wash your hair it is always advisable to spray hair with a leave-in conditioner or moisturizing spray. This will keep your hair from drying out.

Towel dry hair by gently patting dry. Never rub hair shafts together. That causes friction and breakage.

Wet Set. If you don't want to waste time blow drying hair you can either wet set hair like the olden days. It's still in fashion and quite effective. To wet set, apply a styling lotion while hair is wet, use large rollers. (Remember the juice cans?) Magnetic plastic rollers are best. For shorter hair, use pin curls. We used to call these "spit curls" and believe it or not, mama would use her spit in my hair! *Hey, mom's spit could remove rust.*

Blow dryer. It's possible to blow dry your hair straight. Part hair into sections. Carefully comb out each section by starting at the ends and working up. Don't start at the scalp and pull down. Yanking hair could cause breakage. Always use the diffuser. Never blow hair until it's bone dry. Always spritz hair with moisturizer after drying. If at all possible hair should be air-dried as much as possible. Blow-dry when you are going to style hair. To smooth puffy hairline, dab hands with gel smooth hair with hands. If hair is still frizzy, tie scarf around head leave on for 10-15 minutes. Once scarf is removed hair will be flat and smooth.

Curling Iron. If hair is not straight enough for your taste you can use curling iron. It is quite easy and much safer than the old stove method. Remember the smell of the burning hair grease? And who could forget the times of the grease burning your neck? Thank God they've improve this method. Curling iron works great. Use low temperatures and smaller sections than that in blow-drying. You could spritz hair with heat activated styling spray. Section hair; hold iron at roots for a **few seconds** then move the iron slowly along the hair in a straight outward movement. Apply to each section until hair is finished. Style as desired.

Myth #4, Hit the road! A curling iron used sparingly works great to straighten hair.

I don't use hot rollers or hot sticks but if you must use the tissue paper at the ends of your hair for added protection. Do the same for over night sponge rollers.

However you choose to where your hair, be sure that you can master successful hair growth. Being smart, knowing your hair type, applying all the principles in this book, and some from the other Black hair care books, can guarantee accelerated hair growth. Just because you may use products that say it will grow hair, be careful not to believe the hype. You'll never find a quick answer nor a genie in a bottle to give you lush-flowing hair. You have to work at it, like all of us.

It will take a good year or two to see a noticeable amount of hair growth. Six inches in a year, a foot of growth at the end of the second year. Wow, just think, by the end of the third year, you could very possibly see hair down past your bra strap. Hey, it's worth the wait, worth the extra work and way worth the glory that God will give!

And as promised, what I didn't cover in this book, or what I didn't answer concerning your hair personally, check out the appendix for the following Black hair care books. All books can either be purchased on Amazon.com or requested at your local library.

God Bless You and
Happy Hair Growing!!!

Refer to the supplement for a few hairdo ideas from a few sanctified sisters. Pentecostal hairdos look nice on black hair.

With hair, heels, and attitude, honey, I am through the roof!

—RuRaul (1960-)

Quotes from Famous Black Americans

Appendix

Resources for extra tips on great Black hair care
These books are list in the order of which I believe are the most helpful. All books can be purchased at Amazon.com or requested at your local library. There are more hair care books than listed.

1) **Ultra Black Hair Growth II,** Cathy Howse 2000 edition, UBH Publications, Inc. Denver

2) **Good Hair**: For colored girls who've considered weaves when the chemicals became too ruff, Lonnice Brittenum Bonner, Three Rivers Press, New York

3) **Where Beauty Touches Me**: Natural Hair Care and Beauty Book, Pamela Ferrell, Cornrows & Company, Washington, D. C.

4) **Andre Talks Hair**, Andre Walker, Simon & Schuster, New York

5) **Natural Hair Care & Braiding**, Diane Carol Bailey, Salon Ovations, Milady Publishing, New York

6) **Let's Talk Hair**, Pamela Ferrell, Cornrows & Company, Washington, D. C.

7) **Black Woman's Guide to Beautiful Hair**, Lisa Akbari, Sourcebooks, Inc, Naperville

8) **Plaited Glory**, Lonnice Brittenum Bonner, Three Rivers Press, New York

9) **Why Are Black Women Losing Their Hair?,** Barry Fletcher, Unity Publishers, Seat Pleasant, MD

www.ingramcontent.com/pod-product-compliance
Lightning Source LLC
Chambersburg PA
CBHW051954090426
42741CB00008B/1393